Beauty for Ashes
Receiving Emotional Healing

by
Joyce Meyer

Harrison House
Tulsa, Oklahoma

9th Printing

Beauty for Ashes — Receiving Emotional Healing
ISBN 0-89274-679-3
Copyright © 1994 by Joyce Meyer
Life In The Word, Inc.
P. O. Box 655
Fenton, Missouri 63026

Published by Harrison House, Inc.
P. O. Box 35035
Tulsa, Oklahoma 74153

Dedication

I wish to dedicate this book to my husband, Dave, who showed me the love of Jesus while my healing was in progress.

Thank you, Dave, for letting me be me, even when I was not very pleasant; for always being patient and positive, and for trusting God to change me when it looked impossible.

I believe this work is yours as well as mine, and I thank God that He chose to bring you into my life. You truly have always been my "knight in shining armor."

Contents

Foreword

Emotional healing, also referred to as inner healing, is a subject that definitely needs to be talked about. It must, however, be discussed in a scriptural, balanced way that produces godly results.

Our inner life is much more important than our outer life. The Apostle Paul said in 2 Corinthians 4:16 that even though our outer man is (progressively) decaying and wasting away, our inner self is being (progressively) renewed day after day.

Romans 14:17 lets us know that the kingdom of God is not meat and drink (not outward things), but it is righteousness, peace and joy in the Holy Spirit, and Luke 17:21 says the kingdom of God is *within* you.

The summation of what I have learned over the years in this regard is that Jesus is my King. The kingdom He desires to reign over is my inner life — my mind, will, emotions, desires, etc. He brings with Him righteousness, peace and joy. No matter what difficulties or trials I may experience in my outward life, if I am whole inside, I will not only survive, but I will enjoy my life.

Many, many people seem to have it all together outwardly, but inside they are a wreck. That was my situation before I learned that the Lord's main concern is my inner life. Matthew 6:33 states that we are to seek first the kingdom (remember, it is within you) and His righteousness, and *then* these other *things* will be added unto us.

In Isaiah 61 the Lord said that He came to heal the brokenhearted. I believe that means those broken inside, those crushed and wounded inwardly.

7

I believe this book is actually a road map on how to get from devastation to health and wholeness in the inner man. I pray you, the reader, will find it simple, clear and powerful, and that the Holy Spirit will enable you to follow the road map that you may reach your destination.

My prayer for you can be found in Ephesians 3:16 (paraphrased): I pray that you be strengthened in the inner man through the power of the Holy Spirit and that He would indwell your innermost being and personality.

1

Abuse

Some of the terms Webster's Dictionary uses to define "abuse" are: (verb) — "misuse"; "to use wrongly"; "to hurt by treating badly"; "mistreat"; "to use insulting, coarse or bad language about or to"; "revile"; (noun) — "wrong, bad, or excessive use"; "mistreatment"; "injury"; "a bad, unjust, or corrupt custom or practice"; "insulting or coarse language."[1]

I believe that most people are abused in one way or another during their lifetime. Some common forms of abuse are: physical, verbal, emotional and sexual. Whatever form it may take, abuse causes a root of rejection, which is a major problem in our day. God created people for love and acceptance, but the devil works hard to keep us feeling rejected because he knows how rejection injures us emotionally and otherwise.

The above-mentioned types of abuse — whether they take the form of broken relationships, abandonment, divorce, false accusations, exclusion from groups, dislike by teachers and other authority figures, ridicule by peers or any one of hundreds of other such hurtful actions — can and do cause emotional wounds which can hinder people in their efforts to maintain healthy, lasting relationships.

Have you been abused? Misused? Treated wrongly or improperly? Rejected? Has it affected your emotional state? Do you really want to be healed? Do you want to get well?

---

[1]*Webster's New World Dictionary*, 3d college ed., s.v. "abuse."

One of my favorite Scriptures (but a startling one) is John 5:5,6. In this passage Jesus is described as seeing a man lying by the pool of Bethesda who had been sick with a deep-seated and lingering disease for thirty-eight years. Knowing how long this poor man had been in that terrible condition, Jesus asked him, ...**Do you want to become well? [Are you really in earnest about getting well?]** (v. 6).

What kind of a question is that to ask someone who has been hurting for that long? It is a proper question because not everyone wants to get well badly enough to do what is required. Wounded emotions can become a prison that locks self in and others out. Jesus came to open prison doors and to set the captives free! (Luke 4:18.)

This man, like so many people today, had a deep-seated and lingering disorder for a long, long time. After thirty-eight years, he had learned, I am sure, how to function with his disorder. People who are in prison function, but they are not free. However, sometimes prisoners — whether physical or emotional — become so accustomed to being in bondage that they settle in with their condition and learn to live with it.

Are you an "emotional prisoner"? If so, how long have you been in that condition? Is it a deep-seated and lingering disorder? Do you want to be free of it? Do you really want to be well? Jesus wants to heal you. He is willing; are you?

Do You Want To Be Free and Well?

Gaining freedom from emotional bondage is not easy. I will be honest from the beginning and say, point blank, that for many, many people reading this book, it will not be easy. It will provoke feelings and emotions they have been "stuffing" rather than facing and dealing with. You may be one of those people. You may have experienced feelings and emotions in the past that have been too painful to deal with, so each time they have come to the surface you have said to God, "I'm not ready yet, Lord! I'll face that problem later!"

This book will deal not only with the emotional pain caused by what others may have done to you, but also with your responsibility to God for overcoming those traumas and getting well.

Some people (actually a great number of people) have a hard time accepting personal responsibility. In these pages we will deal in a very practical way with forgiveness, repressed anger, self-pity, the chip-on-the-shoulder syndrome, the you-owe-me attitude and many, many other poisonous mental and emotional attitudes that will need cleansing if you are ever to be fully well.

You may be asking, "But, who will deal with the person who hurt me?" We will get around to that issue too. You may also be wondering, "What makes this woman think that she is such an authority on the subject of emotions — especially mine?" You may have questions you would like to ask me, such as: "Do you have a degree in psychology? Where did you do your study? Have you been through any of the things I am going through? How do you know what it is like to be caught in an emotional prison?"

I have answers to all those questions, and if you are brave enough to face your situation and have determined that you really want to get well, then read on.

I Was Abused

My schooling, degrees, experience and qualifications to teach on this subject come from personal experience. I always say, "I graduated from the school of life." I claim the words of the prophet Isaiah as my diploma:

> The Spirit of the Lord God is upon me, because the Lord has anointed and qualified me to preach the Gospel of good tidings to the meek, the poor, and

**afflicted; He has sent me to bind up and heal the
brokenhearted, to proclaim liberty to the [physical and
spiritual] captives, and the opening of the prison and of
the eyes to those who are bound.**

Isaiah 61:1

In verses two and three Isaiah goes on to say:

> **To proclaim the acceptable year of the Lord [the
> year for His favor] and the day of vengeance of our
> God; to comfort all who mourn;**
>
> **To grant [consolation and joy] to those who mourn . . .
> to give them an ornament (a garland or diadem) of** *beauty
> instead of ashes . . . .*

God has exchanged my ashes for beauty and has called me
to help others to learn to allow Him to do the same for them.

I was sexually, physically, verbally and emotionally
abused from the time I can remember until I finally left
home at the age of eighteen. Actually I was abused by
several men in my childhood. I have been rejected,
abandoned, betrayed and divorced. I know what it is to be
an "emotional prisoner."

My purpose in writing this book is not to give my full
testimony in detail. Instead, I want to give you a mini-version
of my own experience so that you will believe that I do know
what it means to hurt and can show you how to recover from
it. I want to help you, and I can do that better if you truly
believe that I understand what you are going through.

Before I begin the details of my childhood and some of
the things I experienced, I wish to say that in no way do I
mean any of these things to be degrading to my parents. I
have learned that hurting people hurt people, that most
people who hurt others have been hurt by someone else.
God has enabled me by His grace to say, "Father, forgive
them, for they really did not know what they were doing." I
tell this story only for the purpose of helping others who,
like me, were abused.

2

Fellowshipping With Fear

Because of the abuse I received at home, my entire childhood was filled with fear. My father controlled me with anger and intimidation. He never physically forced me to submit to him, but he did force me to pretend that I liked what he was doing to me, and that I wanted him to do it. I believe that my inability to express my true feelings about what was happening to me, and my being forced to act as though I enjoyed it, left me with many deep-seated emotional wounds.

The few times I timidly attempted to speak out in honesty about my situation were devastating. My father's violent reaction — his ranting and raving — was so frightening to me that I soon learned just to do whatever he said without objection.

Fear was my constant companion: fear of my father, fear of his anger, fear of being exposed, fear of my mother finding out what was happening, fear of having friends.

My fear of having friends stemmed from two factors: If they were female, I was afraid that my father would attempt to draw them into his trap also. If they were male, I was afraid that my father would harm them or me. He would not permit anyone to come near me because "I belonged to him." He would violently accuse me of being sexually active with male school acquaintances.

All the time I was dealing with a fear of having friends and of being lonely, I was still unwilling to involve anyone else in what was potentially a disaster for them, one that would certainly cause me embarrassment and shame.

I tried to develop acquaintances at school, never allowing the relationships to ripen to the extent that I would be expected to invite my new friends to my home. I would never even allow anyone to feel free to try to contact me there. If the phone rang, and the call was for me, I would panic thinking, "What if it's someone from school?"

Fear! Fear! Fear!

My father drank heavily every weekend, often taking me with him on his drinking bouts and using me at his will. Many times, he would come home angry and beat up my mother. He did not hit me very much, but I imagine that watching him beat my mother was just as damaging as if he had been hitting me.

My father controlled everything that went on around him. He decided what time we got up and when we went to bed; what we ate, wore, and spent; who we associated with; what we watched on television — in short, everything in our lives. He was verbally abusive both to my mother and to me, and eventually to my only brother, who was born when I was nine years old. I remember wanting so desperately for the new baby to be a girl. I thought that maybe if there was another female child in the family I might be left alone, at least part of the time.

My father cursed almost constantly, using extremely vulgar and filthy language. He was critical of everything and everybody. It was his opinion that none of us ever did anything right or that we would ever amount to anything worthwhile. Most of the time, we were reminded that we were "just no good." But there would be moments when he would be just the opposite. He would give us money and tell us to go shopping; sometimes he even bought us presents. He was manipulative and coercive. He did whatever he needed to do in order to get what he wanted. Other people had no value to him at all except to use for his own selfish purposes.

There was no peace in our home. I actually did not know what real peace was until I was grown and had been immersed in the Word of God for many years.

I was born again at the age of nine while visiting relatives out of town. One night I sneaked off from them to attend a church service, intent on finding salvation. I do not even know how I knew I needed to be saved, except that God must have placed that desire within my heart. I did receive Jesus Christ as my Savior that evening and experienced a glorious cleansing. Before that moment I had always felt dirty because of the incest. Now for the first time I felt clean, as though I had received an inner bath. However, since the problem did not go away, once I returned home my old feelings returned. I thought that I had lost Jesus, so I never knew any real inner peace and joy.

The Betrayal

What about my mother? Where did she fit into all this? Why didn't she help me?

I was about eight or nine years old when I told my mother what was going on between my father and me. She examined me and confronted my dad, but he claimed that I was lying — and she chose to believe him rather than me. What woman would not want to believe her husband in such a situation? I think that way down deep inside my mother knew the truth. She just hoped against hope that she was wrong.

When I was fourteen years old, she walked into the house one day, having returned earlier than expected from grocery shopping, and actually caught my father in the act of sexually abusing me. She looked, walked out, and came back two hours later, acting as if she had never been there.

My mother betrayed me.

She did not help me, and she should have.

Many, many years later (actually thirty years later), she confessed to me that she just could not bring herself to face the scandal. She had never mentioned it for thirty years! During that time period she suffered a nervous breakdown. Everyone who knew her blamed it on "the change of life."

For two years she underwent shock treatments, which temporarily erased portions of her memory. None of the doctors knew what they were helping her forget, but they all agreed that she needed to forget something. It was obvious there was something on her mind that was eating away at her mental health.

My mother claimed that her problem was caused by her physical condition. She had an exceptionally hard time during that period of her life due to severe female problems at an earlier age. Following a complete hysterectomy at age thirty-six, she was thrown into premature menopause. At the time, most doctors did not believe in giving hormones to women, so this was a very difficult time for her. It seems that everything in her life combined together was more than she was able to handle.

Personally, I will always believe that my mother's emotional collapse was the result of the years of abuse she had endured, and the truth that she refused to face and deal with. Remember, in John 8:32 our Lord told us: **. . . you will know the Truth, and the Truth will set you free.** God's Word is truth, and, if applied, has inherent power to set a captive free. God's Word also brings us face to face with the issues of our lives. If we choose to turn and run away when the Lord says to stand and confront, *we will stay in bondage.*

Leaving Home

At age eighteen, I moved out while my father was away at work. Shortly thereafter, I married the first young man who showed an interest in me.

Like me, my new husband had lots of problems. He was a manipulator, a thief, and a con man. Most of the time, he did not even work. We moved around a lot, and once he abandoned me in California with nothing but one dime and a carton of soda pop bottles. I was afraid, but since I was accustomed to fear and trauma, I was probably not as affected as someone with less "experience" would have been.

My husband also abandoned me several times simply by leaving during the day while I was at work. Each time he would be gone anywhere from a few weeks to several months. Then he would suddenly reappear, I would listen to his sweet talk and apologies and take him back — only to have the same thing happen all over again. When he was with me, he drank constantly and had relationships with other women regularly.

For five years we played at what we called a marriage. We were both so young, only eighteen, and neither of us had had proper parenting. We were totally ill-equipped to help one another. My problems were only complicated more following a miscarriage at the age of twenty-one, and the birth of my oldest son when I was twenty-two. This event took place during the final year of our marriage. My husband left me and moved in with another woman who lived two blocks from our place, telling anyone who would listen that the child I was carrying was not his.

I remember coming dangerously close to losing my mind during that summer of 1965. Throughout my pregnancy, I lost weight because I could not eat. Without friends, money, or insurance, I went through a hospital clinic, seeing a different doctor each time I had a checkup. Actually, the doctors I saw were interns in training. I was unable to sleep, so I began taking over-the-counter sleeping pills. Thank God, they did not harm me or my unborn child.

The temperature that summer rose to more than a hundred degrees, and there was no fan or air-conditioning in my third-floor, attic apartment. My only material possession was an old Studebaker automobile that got vapor lock on a regular basis. Since my father had always insisted that some day I would need his help and come crawling back to him, I was determined to do anything but that — even though I did not know what it would be.

I can remember being under such mental strain that I would sit and stare at the walls or out the window for hours, not even realizing what I was doing. I worked until my baby was due. When I had to quit my job, my hairdresser and her mother took me in. My baby was four and a half weeks late. I had no idea what to expect, and no notion of how to care for him when he was born. When the baby did come, my husband showed up at the hospital. Since the baby looked so much like him, there was no way he could deny that it was his. Once again he said he was sorry and that he was going to change.

When it was time for me to be discharged from the hospital, we had no place to live, so my husband contacted his brother's ex-wife, who was a wonderful Christian woman, and she let us live with her for a while until I was able to go back to work.

I think you can imagine from these few details what my life was like. Actually it was ridiculous! There was nothing stable in my entire existence, and stability was something that I needed and craved desperately.

Finally, in the summer of 1966, I reached the point of not caring what happened to me. I could not stand the thought of staying with my husband any longer. I did not have one ounce of respect for the man, especially since, to top it all off, by this time he was in trouble with the law. I took my son, and what I could carry, and walked out. I went to a corner phone booth where I called my dad and asked him if I could come home. Of course, he was delighted!

After I had lived at home for a couple of months, I learned that my divorce had been granted. That was in September of 1966. By that time my mother's mental health was growing worse by the day. She had begun to have violent fits, accusing store clerks of robbing her, threatening the people she worked with over meaningless details. She even started carrying a knife in her purse. She ranted and raved about anything and everything. I distinctly remember one night when she beat me with a broom because I had failed to mop the bathroom floor! While all this was going on, I made an occupation of steering clear of my father. As much as possible, I avoided being left alone with him.

In short, my life was a living hell.

For "entertainment," I began to go to bars on weekends. I suppose I was looking for someone to love me. I would have a few drinks, but rarely ever enough to get drunk. I really had never cared much for drinking. I also refused to sleep with the various men I met. Even though my life was a mess, there was a deep desire in me to be good and pure.

Confused, afraid, lonely, discouraged and depressed, I often prayed, "Dear God, please let me be happy . . . someday. Give me someone who will really love me — and make it someone who will take me to church."

My Knight in Shining Armor

My parents owned and resided in a two-family apartment. One of their renters worked with a man named Dave Meyer. One evening Dave came by to pick up his friend to go bowling. I was washing my mother's car. He saw me and tried to flirt with me, but I was my usual sarcastic self. He asked me if I wanted to wash his car when I was finished with mine, and I replied, "If you want your car washed, wash it yourself!" Because of my experience with my father and my former husband, I didn't trust men at all, and that is an understatement!

Dave, however, was being totally led by the Spirit of God. Born again and baptized in the Holy Spirit, he loved God with all his heart. At twenty-six years of age, he was also ready to get married and had been praying for six months that God would lead him to the right woman. He had even asked the Lord for her to be someone who needed help!

Since Dave was being led by the Lord, my sarcasm, instead of insulting him, only served to encourage him. Later he told his friend from work that he would like to have a date with me. At first I refused, but later I changed my mind. We had been out on five dates when Dave asked me to marry him. He told me that he had known the first night we went out together that he wanted me to be his wife, but that he had decided to wait a few weeks before proposing marriage, lest he frighten me.

For my part, I certainly did not know what love was, and was not eager to get involved with another man. However, since things were getting even worse at home, and since I was living in total panic all the time, I decided that anything would be better than what I was going through at the moment.

Dave asked me if I would go to church with him, which I was willing to do. Remember, one of my prayer requests had been that when the Lord gave me someone to love me, he would be a person who would take me to church. I strongly desired to live a Christian life, but I knew that I needed someone strong to lead the way. Dave also promised to be good to my little boy, who was ten months old when we met. I had named him David, which was what my brother was called, and my favorite name for a boy. I am still amazed at the way the Lord was working out a plan for my good, right in the midst of my darkest despair.

Dave and I were married on January 7, 1967, but we did not live "happily ever after"! Marriage did not solve my problems, and neither did going to church. My problems were not in my home life or my marriage, but in me, in my wounded, crippled emotions.

Abuse leaves a person emotionally handicapped, unable to maintain healthy, lasting relationships. I wanted to give and receive love, but I couldn't. Like my father, I was controlling, manipulative, angry, critical, negative, overbearing and judgmental. All that I had grown up with, I had become. Filled with self-pity, I was verbally abusive, depressed and bitter. I could go on and on describing my personality, but I am sure you get the picture.

I functioned in society. I worked; Dave worked. We went to church together. We got along part of the time, only then because Dave was extremely easy going. He usually let me have my way, but when he didn't it made me mad. As far as I was concerned, I was right about everything. To me, I didn't have a problem; everyone else did.

Now remember, I was born again. I loved Jesus. I believed that my sins were forgiven and that I would go to heaven when I died. But I knew no victory, no peace or joy in my everyday life. Although I believed that Christians were supposed to be happy, I certainly wasn't! I didn't even know what righteousness, imputed through the blood of Jesus, was. I felt condemned all the time. I was out of control. The only time I didn't hate myself was when I was working toward some personal goal which I thought would provide me a sense of self-worth.

I kept thinking that if *things* would change, if *other people* would change, then I would be all right. If my husband, my kids, my finances, my health, were different; if I could go on vacation, get a new car, buy a new dress; if I could get out of the house, find a job, earn more money, then I would be happy and fulfilled. I was always doing what is described in Jeremiah 2:13; I was digging wells that had no water in them.

I was making the frustrating, tragic mistake of trying to find the kingdom of God (which according to Romans 14:17 is righteousness, peace, and joy) in things and other people. What I did not realize is that, as Jesus taught us in Luke 17:20,21, and as the Apostle Paul pointed out in his letter to the Colossians, the kingdom is within us: . . . **Christ in you, the hope of glory** (Col. 1:27 KJV). My joy had to be found "in Him," but it took me years and years to find that out.

I tried to earn righteousness by being good, through works of the flesh. I was on the evangelism committee and the church board. My husband was an elder in the church. Our children went to parochial school. I tried to do all the right things. I tried and tried and tried, and yet it seemed that I just could not keep myself from making mistakes. I was worn out and burned out, frustrated and miserable!

I Was Sincerely
Ignorant of the Problem

It never occurred to me that I was suffering from the years of abuse and rejection I had gone through. I thought that all that was behind me. It was true that it was no longer happening to me physically, but it was all recorded in my emotions and in my mind. I still felt the effects of it, and I still acted them out.

I needed emotional healing!

Legally, I was a new creature in Christ (2 Cor. 5:17), but experientially, I had not yet taken hold of the new creation reality. I lived out of my own mind, will and emotions, which were all damaged. Jesus had paid the price for my total deliverance, but I had no idea how to receive His gracious gift.

3

Addictive Behavior
Caused by Abuse

The first thing to realize is that the fruit in our lives (our behavior) comes from somewhere. A person who is violent is that way for a reason. His behavior is the bad fruit of a bad tree with bad roots. As I always say, *"Rotten fruit comes from rotten roots; good fruit comes from good roots."*

It is important to take a close look at your roots. If they were unpleasant, harmful or abusive, the good news is that you can be uprooted from that bad soil and be transplanted into the good soil of Christ Jesus, so that you become rooted and grounded in Him and in His love. (Eph. 3:17; Col. 2:7 KJV.)

Jesus will graft you into Himself. As you, a branch, are grafted into Him, the Root and Vine (John 15:5), you will begin to receive all the "sap" (all the riches of His love and grace) which flow from Him. In other words, if while you were growing up you did not receive what you needed to make you sound and healthy, Jesus will gladly give it to you now.

In my own life there was a lot of bad fruit, which I kept trying to get rid of. I worked hard at trying to behave correctly. Yet it seemed that no matter what kind of bad behavior I tried to get rid of, two or three others popped up somewhere else. It was like dandelions or weeds. I kept pulling off the visible part, but was not getting to the hidden root of the problem. The root was alive and kept producing a new crop of problems.

Does this scenario sound familiar?

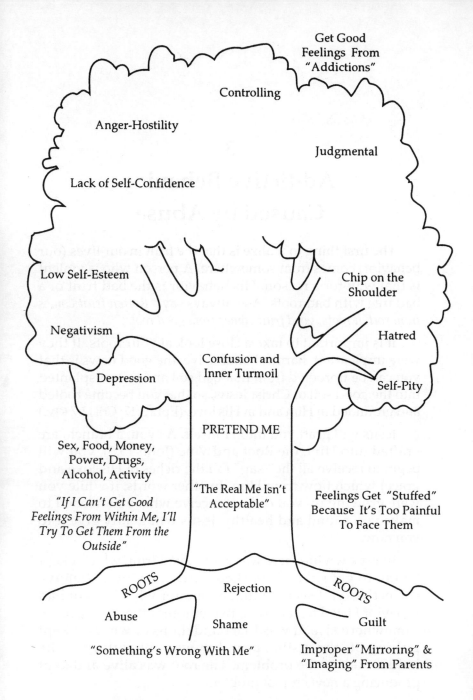

Get Good
Feelings From
"Addictions"

Controlling

Anger-Hostility

Judgmental

Lack of Self-Confidence

Low Self-Esteem

Chip on the
Shoulder

Negativism

Hatred

Confusion and
Inner Turmoil

Depression

Self-Pity

PRETEND ME

Sex, Food, Money,
Power, Drugs,
Alcohol, Activity

"The Real Me Isn't
Acceptable"

Feelings Get "Stuffed"
Because It's Too Painful
To Face Them

*"If I Can't Get Good
Feelings From Within Me, I'll
Try To Get Them From the
Outside"*

ROOTS

Rejection

ROOTS

Abuse

Guilt

Shame

"Something's Wrong With Me"

Improper "Mirroring" &
"Imaging" From Parents

Rotten fruit comes from rotten roots.

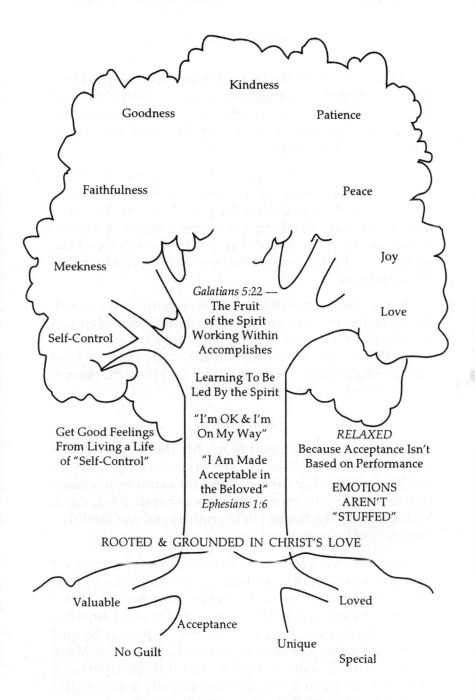

Kindness

Goodness   Patience

Faithfulness   Peace

Meekness   Joy

Love

Galatians 5:22 —
The Fruit
of the Spirit
Working Within
Accomplishes

Self-Control

Learning To Be
Led By the Spirit

"I'm OK & I'm
Get Good Feelings   On My Way"
From Living a Life   *RELAXED*
of "Self-Control"   "I Am Made   Because Acceptance Isn't
                            Acceptable in   Based on Performance
                            the Beloved"
                            Ephesians 1:6   EMOTIONS
                                                    AREN'T
                                                    "STUFFED"

ROOTED & GROUNDED IN CHRIST'S LOVE

Valuable   Loved

Acceptance

No Guilt   Unique
                                    Special

Good fruit comes from good roots.

As an illustration, the Lord gave me this example. Have you ever opened the refrigerator door and noticed a stink? You knew that there was something spoiled in there, but in order to find out what was causing the smell, you had to remove everything in the refrigerator.

The same principle applies to your personal life. If you are having emotional problems, it may be because there is something spoiled deep within you. You may have to do some searching, some emptying out and even some taking apart in order to get to the source of the problem and remove it so that everything can be made fresh and new.

Remember, uprooting can be traumatic and painful. Being replanted, becoming rooted and grounded is a process that takes time. It is by faith and patience that we inherit God's promises (Heb. 6:12), so be patient. God always finishes what He begins. (Phil 1:6.) He is the Author and the Finisher. (Heb. 12:2.)

Bad Fruit

I had so much bad fruit in my life that I experienced regular bouts of depression, negativism, self-pity, quick temper and the chip-on-the-shoulder syndrome. I had a controlling, domineering spirit. I was harsh, hard, rigid, legalistic and judgmental. I held grudges and was fearful — especially of being rejected.

I was one person on the inside and another on the outside. I pretended to be very confident, and in some ways I was. Still, I had very low self-esteem, and my so-called confidence was not really based on who I was in Christ but on the approval of others, on my appearance and accomplishments and on other such external factors. Many people think they are confident, but if their superficial exterior is stripped away, they are actually scared stiff! I was confused and full of inner turmoil.

I am extremely blessed to be able to say that I never became addicted to drugs or alcohol. I smoked cigarettes, but had no other chemical dependencies. I just plain did not like alcohol. I would take a few drinks, but as soon as I started feeling woozy, I would never drink beyond that point.

I always had a lot of self-control. It was part of my personality not to let anything control me, so I stayed away from drugs. I think the fact that my father had controlled my life so long fostered a determination in me that nothing else would. Although I could not control my inner problems, I seemed to have a certain wisdom about staying away from things that could render me dependent upon them.

I took diet pills once because I was always about twenty-five pounds overweight. Although they were prescribed by a doctor, they made me "high." They were amphetamines, but I had no idea they were harmful. I loved the way they made me feel all day! When I was on them, I could work like a machine, clean house, be creative and friendly; I was up, up, up. But when they wore off, I was worn out!

Although I didn't lose any weight, the pills did take care of my appetite — until they wore off. I would not eat all day, but at night I would feel so down that I would make up for what I had missed throughout the day. I remember debating about whether I should get the prescription refilled, but I had a "knowing" inside that I would get addicted to the pills if I kept taking them, so I just quit.

I realize now that the ability to avoid things that could have destroyed me came as a result of having received Jesus when I was nine years old. Even though I did not know how to develop a real relationship with the Lord, He was always with me and helping me in ways I did not recognize at the time for lack of knowledge. Years later, these blessings were made very clear to me.

I know that God's grace and mercy kept me from serious problems such as crime, drugs, alcoholism and prostitution. I am grateful to the Lord and still in awe of how He kept me. Although I did not have those kinds of problems, I had plenty of others. Bad roots had caused my bad fruit.

Pretending

I was so miserable and unhappy. Yet, like so many people, I pretended that everything was fine. We human beings pretend for the benefit of others, not wanting them to know about our misery, but we also pretend for ourselves so that we do not have to face and deal with difficult issues.

I don't think I ever realized just how miserable I really was until I had spent some time in the Word of God and had begun to experience some emotional healing. If a person has never known true happiness, how can he know what he is missing? I don't remember ever being fully relaxed and truly happy as a child. I don't believe that anyone can enjoy life while living in constant fear.

I recall Dave talking about his childhood one evening after we were married. He grew up with seven brothers and sisters. They had so much love in their home and a lot of fun as children — summers spent in the country, picnics, ball games, friends and a Christian mother who played with them and taught them about Jesus. They did not have much money because Dave's father had died from liver disease brought on by alcoholism. Yet the influence, prayers and Christian example of Dave's mother kept the family out of trouble.

They had love, which is what all of us need and are actually created for.

As Dave shared with me that evening about all the good times he and his family had and how much he enjoyed his youthful years, I suddenly had a realization that I did not like. I could never, *ever* remember being happy as a child! Something had been stolen from me that I could never get back. I felt terribly cheated. Perhaps you feel the same way. If so, God will do for you what He has done for me. He will make it up to you. He will, Himself, be your reward and will recompense you for what you have lost.

I realized that I had to stop pretending and face the truth. I had some addictive behaviors from my past. That past was not Dave's fault, nor my children's fault. It was unfair to continue making them suffer for something in which they had, had no part.

Addictive Behaviors

Addictive behaviors that can develop from abuse are probably endless, but here is a partial list:

Substance abuse
Alcohol
Drugs (illegal and prescription)

Obsession with money
Excessive spending
Hoarding

Food disorders
Bulimia (binge-purge)
Anorexia (self-starvation)
Obesity caused by gluttony

Note: Some people who have been promiscuous stay fat on purpose in order to avoid being attractive. They fear falling back into temptation. Those who have been deprived of love may eat to make up to themselves for what they have missed.

Feeling addictions

Rage

Sadness

Fear

Excessive excitement

Religious righteousness

Joy fixation (wearing a continuous, frozen smile; never appearing to be angry; laughing at inappropriate times; speaking only of happy things)

Thought addictions

Detailing

Worry

Non-stop talking

Lustful thoughts

Unsettled mind (never at rest; always figuring out what to say and do, how to react, etc.)

Activity obsessions

Work

Sports

Reading

Gambling

Exercise

Television viewing

Owning and caring for excessive numbers of pets

Will addictions

Controlling — Controlling people feel they must have their way in every situation. They cannot submit emotion to logic or reason. They feel safe only when they are in control.

Controlled — Those controlled become so passive, they give their will over to people and do whatever anyone says. They can even become possessed or severely oppressed by giving their will to the devil. They are so shame-based, they feel they deserve nothing — not even choice.

Re-enactment addicts — These addicts re-enact their own abuse on their children or repeatedly put themselves in situations as adults that produce the same type of thing that happened to them as a child. A similar scene gives "flashbacks," and they take on the role of the abuser so as not to feel the painful memories of abuse.

Example: A man who was beaten by his father in childhood may physically abuse his own children as a result of seeing "flashbacks" of the old scene and assuming the role of abuser rather than waiting to be abused himself. A woman who was physically, sexually or verbally abused by her father may marry a man, or even several men in succession, who will treat her in the same way. She may feel that she is not worthy of anything else or that she deserves being mistreated. She may even see to it that she receives her mistreatment, perhaps even provoking the one who will abuse her.

Caretaker — Some people find their worth in caring for others who need them. They feel so worthless that they become addicted to caretaking, helping, people-pleasing and being nice because doing so makes them feel good.

Created To Feel Good Inside

As human beings we are created by God to be happy and to feel good (right) about ourselves. As a matter of fact, we must feel good about ourselves or eventually we will develop some sort of uncontrolled behavior, because such behavior gives us "good feelings," even if only for a little while.

Think about it. A person addicted to drugs probably got started because his pain was so intense he felt compelled to get rid of it and feel good ("high"), even if only temporarily. The same thing is prevalent with drinking. Food is also used by many people as a comfort. Eating is enjoyable; it makes us feel good while we are engaging in it. Many people who have eating disorders are starving for love. They want to feel good about themselves. If we do not get good feelings from the inside, then we will get them from somewhere else.

If you have any addictive behaviors, this chapter may help you to understand the root of the problem. You can spend your entire life dealing with the outward behavior (the bad fruit), but it will come out somewhere else if the root has not been taken care of.

4
Loved at Last

If you are a person who has been abused, by now you have probably identified some problem areas in your life. To point out problems without offering a solution to them would be disastrous. If I did that, you would end up more frustrated than you were before you began reading this book.

I intend to outline the major truths that brought healing in my own life. As I do so, I would like to remind you that, according to the Apostle Peter, . . . **God is no respecter of persons** (Acts 10:34 KJV). What He does for one, He will do for another, if it is a promise found in His Word.

The Process of Healing

My first husband did not know how to love, so I received no love at all from our relationship. Although my wonderful second husband, Dave, did truly love me, I knew no more than I ever had about how to receive love. I bounced back and forth between: (1) rejecting his love and closing him out of my life by building walls around myself to ensure that I would not get hurt (or so I thought), and, (2) trying to get him to love me with a kind of perfect and complete love that was humanly impossible for him to achieve.

In 1 John 4:18 we read that perfect love casts out fear. Only God can love perfectly and without fault. No matter how much anyone may love another person, he is still human. As our Lord said, . . . **the spirit indeed is willing,**

but the flesh is weak (Matt. 26:41 KJV). People always disappoint other people — they always love somewhat imperfectly, simply because that is part of human nature.

I was trying to get Dave to give me something that only God could give me, which was a sense of my own value and worth. I wanted my husband to love me totally and to treat me perfectly so I could finally feel good about myself. Whenever he failed me, disappointed me or hurt me, I would put up walls between us and not allow him in at all for days or even weeks.

Many people from abusive, dysfunctional backgrounds cannot maintain healthy, lasting relationships because either they don't know how to receive love or they place an unbalanced demand on their marriage partners to give them what only God can give. The resulting frustration often ruins the marriage.

This same principle can be applied to friendships. One time a woman came up to me in a prayer line and said: "Joyce, help me. I am so lonely. Every time I get a friend, I suffocate them." This lady was so love-starved that if she found anyone who would pay any attention to her at all, she tried to collect all her past emotional debts from that individual, who owed her nothing. Her new friend was usually frightened away.

God's Boundless, Unconditional, Perfect Love

One day as I was reading the Bible, I noticed this statement in 2 Corinthians 5:7: **For we walk by faith [we regulate our lives and conduct ourselves by our conviction or belief respecting man's relationship to God and divine things, with trust and holy fervor; thus we walk] not by sight or appearance.**

There the Holy Spirit stopped me and asked, "What do you believe, Joyce, about your relationship with God? Do you believe He loves you?"

As I honestly began to search my heart and to study the Word of God on this subject, I came to the conclusion that I did believe that God loved me, but *conditionally*.

The Bible teaches us that God loves us perfectly or unconditionally. His perfect love for us is not based on our perfection. It is not based on anything except Himself. God is love. (1 John 4:8.) Love is not His occupation; it is Who He is. God is always loving us, but often we stop *receiving* His love, especially if our behavior is not good.

I would like to stop here and present several passages of Scripture that have come to mean a lot to me. Please take time to read them slowly. Digest them and allow them to become a part of you:

> And we know (understand, recognize, are conscious of, by observation and by experience), and believe (adhere to and put faith in and rely on) the *love* God cherishes for us. God is *love*, and he who dwells and continues in *love* dwells and continues in God, and God dwells and continues in him.
>
> In this [union and communion with Him] *love* is brought to completion and attains perfection with us, that we may have confidence for the day of judgment [with assurance and boldness to face Him], because as He is, so are we in this world.
>
> There is no fear in *love* [dread does not exist], but full-grown (complete, perfect) *love* turns fear out of doors and expels every trace of terror! For fear brings with it the thought of punishment, and [so] he who is afraid has not reached the full maturity of *love* [is not yet grown into love's complete perfection].
>
> We *love* Him, because He first *loved* us.
>
> **1 John 4:16-19**

In this the *love* of God was made manifest (displayed) where we are concerned: in that God sent His Son, the only begotten or unique [Son], into the world so that we might live through Him.

In this is *love:* not that we *loved* God, but that He *loved* us and sent His Son to be the propitiation (the atoning sacrifice) for our sins.

Beloved, if God *loved* us so [very much], we also ought to *love* one another.

1 John 4:9-11

Who shall ever separate us from Christ's *love*? Shall suffering and affliction and tribulation? Or calamity and distress? Or persecution or hunger or destitution or peril or sword?

Romans 8:35

For I am persuaded beyond doubt (am sure) that neither death nor life, nor angels nor principalities, nor things impending and threatening nor things to come, nor powers,

Nor height nor depth, nor anything else in all creation will be able to separate us from the *love* of God which is in Christ Jesus our Lord.

Romans 8:38,39

May Christ through your faith [actually] dwell (settle down, abide, make His permanent home) in your hearts! May you be rooted deep in *love* and founded securely on *love,*

That you may have the power and be strong to apprehend and grasp with all the saints [God's devoted people, the experience of that *love*] what is the breadth and length and height and depth [of it];

[That you may really come] to know [practically, through experience for yourselves] the *love* of Christ, which far surpasses mere knowledge [without experience]; that you may be filled [through all your being] unto all the fullness of God [may have the richest measure of the divine Presence, and become a body wholly filled and flooded with God Himself]!

Ephesians 3:17-19

Such hope never disappoints or deludes or shames us, for God's *love* has been poured out in our hearts through the Holy Spirit Who has been given to us.
Romans 5:5

Behold, I have indelibly imprinted (tattooed a picture of) you on the palm of each of My hands. . . .
Isaiah 49:16

First John 4:16 was a key Scripture for me because it says that *we should be conscious and aware of God's love and put faith in it.* I was unconscious and unaware of God's love; therefore, I was not putting faith in His love for me.

When the devil condemned me, I did not know how to say, "Yes, I made a mistake," then go to God, ask for His forgiveness, receive His love, and press on. Instead, I would spend hours and even days feeling guilty about each little thing I did wrong. I was literally tormented! John tells us that fear has torment, but that the perfect love of God casts out fear. (1 John 4:18.) God's love for me was perfect because it was based on Him, not on me. So even when I failed, He kept loving me.

God's love for you is perfect — and unconditional. When you fail, He keeps on loving you because His love is not based on you but on Him. When you fail, do you stop receiving God's love and start punishing yourself by feeling guilty and condemned? I felt guilty and bad about myself for the first forty years of my life. I faithfully carried my sack of guilt on my back everywhere I went. It was a heavy burden, and it was always with me. I made mistakes regularly, and I felt guilty about each one of them.

In Romans 8:33-35 the Apostle Paul says:

Who shall bring any charge against God's elect [when it is] God Who justifies [that is, Who puts us in right relation to Himself? Who shall come forward and accuse or impeach those whom God has chosen? Will God, Who acquits us?]

Who is there to condemn [us]? Will Christ Jesus (the Messiah), Who died, or rather Who was raised from the dead, Who is at the right hand of God actually pleading as He intercedes for us?

Who shall ever separate us from Christ's love?. . . .

You see, the devil's goal is to separate us from God's love, because *God's love is the main factor in our emotional healing.*

We are created for love. In Ephesians 2:4-6 Paul says that God is so rich in mercy that He saved us and gave us what we do not deserve, in order to satisfy the demands of His *intense* love for us. Think about it. God intends to love us. He *has* to love us — He *is* love!

You and I are created for love! Sin separated us from God, but He loved us so much that He sent His only Son, Jesus, to die for us, to redeem us, to purchase us back, so that He could lavish His great love upon us. All we need to do is begin to believe what the Bible says about our relationship with God. Once we do that, the healing process can start.

During the first year that my husband Dave and I began our ministry called Life In The Word, the Holy Spirit worked with teaching me about God's love. I kept a book of remembrance of special things the Lord did for me during that time — little things mostly, personal things that showed me that God cared. By this method I began to become more conscious of His unconditional love. It helped me to remember that God loved me.

If you can believe that God, Who is so perfect, loves you, then you can believe that you are worth loving.

Once you begin believing that you are accepted and loved by God, then you can begin accepting and loving yourself. Then not only will you start loving God in return, but you will also start loving other people.

You Can't Give Away
What You Don't Have!

Many people receive Jesus and then immediately start trying to love everybody. Too often they end up feeling condemned because they find that they just can't do it. It is impossible to truly love others without first receiving the love of God, because there is no love there to give.

In the thirteenth chapter of 1 Corinthians, often called "the love chapter," Paul emphasizes this truth quite clearly. In verse 1 he defines love as . . . **(that reasoning, intentional, spiritual devotion** *such as is inspired by God's love for and in us)***. . . .** This entire chapter is focused on teaching us how to walk in love, yet it clearly says that love must first be in us.

Most people can believe that God loves them when they can feel that they deserve it. Problems arise when they feel that they do not deserve God's love, and yet desperately need it.

The following charts illustrate the ongoing effects of receiving or not receiving the love of God. Notice that the belief that God's love for us depends on our worthiness is a deception that causes *many* problems in our lives. On the other hand, believing that God loves us unconditionally brings much joy and blessedness.

Receiving God's Love

I suggest that you determine that you are going to receive God's love. Here are some practical suggestions to help you do that. These are all things that I believe the Lord led me to do, and I believe they will be of help to you too. However, remember that we are all special and unique and that God has an individual, personalized plan for each of us.

Don't get lost in methods.

The Trickle-Down Theory of Unconditional Love

Jesus loves me, this I know.
He loves me unconditionally.

THEREFORE: His love for me is based on who *HE* is.

THEREFORE: I have not earned His love, nor can I earn His love.

THEREFORE: I cannot be separated from His love.
When I obey Him, He will bless me.
When I disobey Him, there will be consequences for my behavior.
He may not like my behavior, but he always loves me.

THEREFORE: Since I have experienced God's love, I know I am loveable.

THEREFORE, since I know that God loves me, I am able to believe that there are people who could love me, too.

THEREFORE, I am able to trust people who genuinely love me.

THEREFORE, I am able to accept the love that those people give to me.

THEREFORE, since my most basic need for love and a sense of self-worth have been met by God, I don't need to be "fixed" by other people.

THEREFORE, although I have needs that I look to other people to meet, I believe those needs are balanced and God-given (i.e., companionship, affection, fun). I try to be honest in assessing those needs and in asking for what I need.

THEREFORE, I expect other people to be honest with me. I can handle criticism or confrontation if it is done with love.

THEREFORE, since I know that I am God's special and unique creation, I know that the love I have to give is valuable.

THEREFORE, I don't feel that I have to "perform" for other people. They will either love me for who I am or they won't. It's important for me to be loved for who I am.

THEREFORE, I am able to get my mind off of what others are thinking *ABOUT ME* and focus on other people and *THEIR NEEDS*.

THEREFORE, I am able to sustain a healthy, loving, lasting relationship.

The Trickle-Down Theory of Conditional Love

Jesus loves me, but . . .

He loves me conditionally.

THEREFORE: His love is based on my performance.

THEREFORE: I have to earn His love by pleasing Him.

THEREFORE: When I please Him, I feel loved.

When I don't please Him, I feel rejected.

THEREFORE: If God, Who is "all-loving," does not always love, accept and value me, how can I be expected to believe that I am valuable and loveable?

THEREFORE: I don't believe that I am basically a loveable, valuable person.

THEREFORE, I am not able to trust other people who say they love me. I suspect their motives or figure that they just don't know the "real" me yet.

THEREFORE, I can't accept love from other people. I deflect it. I try to prove that I am right — that I am NOT loveable, and that they will eventually reject me.

THEREFORE, they usually do.

THEREFORE, I use the world's standards (money, status, clothes, etc.) to prove to myself and others that I am *VALUABLE*. I need strokes and feed back from other people to prove to myself and to others that I am *LOVEABLE*.

THEREFORE, I need a "fresh fix" of strokes every day just to get through the day feeling good about myself.

THEREFORE, I look to others to give me something that only God can give me — a sense of my own *SELF-WORTH*.

THEREFORE, I place impossible demands on people who love me. I frustrate them. I am never satisfied with what they are giving me. I don't allow them to be honest with me or confront me. I'm focused on me, and I expect them to be focused on me, too.

THEREFORE, since I don't love who I AM, I don't expect that others will love me either. Why would anyone want something that has no real value.

THEREFORE, I try to earn their love by what I *DO*. I don't give out of a desire to love, but to *BE LOVED*. Most of what I do is tied up in "self," so the people I profess to love don't really feel loved. They feel manipulated. I'm trying to avoid rejection rather than trying to build a loving relationship.

THEREFORE: I am not able to sustain a healthy, loving, lasting relationship.

1. Tell yourself, in your mind and out loud, "God loves me." Say it, and let it sink in. Repeat it often: when you awaken in the morning, when you go to bed at night and throughout the entire day. Look at yourself in the mirror, point to yourself, call yourself by name and say, "_____, God loves you."

2. Keep a diary, a book of remembrance of special things that God does for you. Include little things as well as major things. Read over your list at least once a week and you will be encouraged. Let this become a Holy Ghost project. I think you will have fun with it — I did.

3. Learn and even commit to memory several Scriptures about the love of God for you.

4. Read some good books about God's love. I recommend that you start with the one I have written called *Tell Them I Love Them.**

5. Pray for the Holy Spirit, Who is the Teacher, to give you a revelation of God's love.

---

*I also have available a Scripture and music tape entitled "Healing the Brokenhearted" that will help you have a healthy self-image.

5

Learn To Follow the Holy Spirit

When people arrive at the conclusion that they need emotional healing, and that many of the problems they face are a result of bad roots from the past, often they are anxious to get rid of those roots of the problem so they can be made well.

That is understandable, but it is important to allow the Holy Spirit to lead, guide and direct you in that healing process. God has already sent Jesus Christ to come to earth and purchase your complete healing. Once that was accomplished, He sent His Holy Spirit to administer to you what was bought by the blood of His Son.

In John 16:7 Jesus told His disciples that it was better for them that He go away to be with the Father, because if He did not go, the Comforter could not come. The Comforter is the Holy Spirit. In *The Amplified Bible* version of this verse He is called the Counselor, Helper, Advocate, Intercessor, Strengthener and Standby. During your recovery process, you will need to experience every facet of the Holy Spirit's ministry.

Seek Only Godly Counsel

Don't run around seeking counsel from just anyone. Pray first, asking the Lord whether it is His will that you go to another human being for counsel or whether He desires to counsel you Himself.

In my own life I have had many, many problems, yet I never went to anyone else for counsel with the exception of one time. On this occasion I visited a lady in ministry who had been abused herself. I do not mean to discredit her, but she really was not able to help me. It was not her fault; she simply was not anointed by the Lord to help me.

God is not obligated to anoint what He does not initiate.

So often people run to others without following the guidance and leadership of the Holy Spirit, and it never bears good, lasting fruit.

When you are in trouble, go to the Throne before you go to the phone.

I do not mean to suggest that it is wrong to seek counsel. I am just suggesting that you pray and allow the Lord to lead and guide you through the Holy Spirit. Let Him choose the right counsellor for you. Just because a person has been through what you are going through or is a close personal friend does not mean that individual is the right counsellor for you. So I repeat, *pray!*

I am definitely *not* saying that you should not seek counsel just because I didn't. We all have different personalities. I happen to have a strong, determined, self-disciplined, goal-oriented personality. These traits helped me to keep moving toward my objective, which was emotional wholeness. Others may need someone to help them along a bit, someone to assist them in setting goals for themselves and to keep striving toward those goals.

It is vital to follow the leading of the Holy Spirit. He is the best Counsellor. Either He will help you directly or He will guide you to someone through whom He can minister to you. In either case, you should ultimately look to Him for your help. Even the counsel that other people may offer you will not become *rhema* (personal revelation from God) to you without the help of the Holy Spirit.

It is also important to realize that God has different calls on our lives. Since He has called me to teach His Word, it was better for me to receive the truth I needed directly from Him. However, that is not a rule for everyone.

The Ministry of the Holy Spirit

Another reason the ministry of the Holy Spirit is so important is found in John 16:8 in which Jesus says that it is the Holy Spirit Who convicts and convinces of sin and of righteousness.

Most people who have been abused are shame-based individuals. (The topic of shame will be discussed in detail in a later chapter.) They feel bad about themselves. They don't like themselves, and therefore they experience a lot of guilt and condemnation.

It is the devil who brings condemnation; the Holy Spirit brings conviction. (There is a difference. I welcome conviction, but I resist condemnation — and so should you.) Only the Holy Spirit, through the Word of God and His power to change, can convince a shame-based person that he has been made righteous through the shed blood of Jesus Christ. (2 Cor. 5:21.)

In John 16:13 Jesus refers to the Holy Spirit as the Spirit of Truth and assures us that He will guide us . . . **into** *all* **the Truth — the whole, full Truth.** . . . In John 14:26 He says that the Holy Spirit will prompt our memory. Both of these aspects of the ministry of the Spirit are major areas of assistance for those who are in recovery from abuse. Such people must get out of their denial and face the truth. There may be things they have forgotten because they are too painful to remember, things that will have to be recalled and faced during the healing process.

If the person in charge of the recovery is not led by the Spirit, he sometimes can take the abused person through the process too quickly. If too accelerated, it can become more painful than the person can handle.

I remember a girl who once came to me in a prayer line. She was very upset and extremely emotional, almost panic-stricken. She began to relate to me that every week when she went to visit her counsellor, it was so painful that it was almost more than she could bear. In her anxiety, I heard her say several times, "It's just too much. It hurts so bad, I can't stand it."

At the time she was speaking, I was praying and asking the Lord to help me so I could help her. I was actually concerned that she might become hysterical right there at the altar. Suddenly I received an answer from the Lord. I felt that probably her counsellor was not sensitive to the Spirit and that she was having this young woman face issues so fast that her mind and her emotional system were unable to handle it all.

When I said to her, "Listen to me, I think I know what the problem is," she quieted down long enough for me to share what God was saying. As she listened, she immediately began to get some relief. She agreed that what I was describing was exactly what was happening.

During my own healing process, the Holy Spirit led me to many different things. The first was a book that my husband suggested I read. It was the testimony of a woman who had been abused as a child. Until that time, I did not think that any of my problems were a result of my past. I thought that everyone had such problems.

That book was so difficult for me to read. When I came to the part in which the woman began describing in detail how her stepfather had sexually abused her, the memories, pain, anger and rage began rushing up in me from somewhere deep inside. I threw that book on the floor and loudly exclaimed, "I will not read this!"

Just then I heard the Holy Spirit reply, "It is time."

I had been attempting to walk with God for several years when this event took place. Why hadn't He led me to something that could have helped me sooner? Because *it wasn't time*! The Holy Spirit knows precisely the right timing in our lives. I always say, "Only the Spirit knows when you are ready for what." In other words, the Spirit of the Lord is the only One Who knows what it will take to help you, and when you are ready to receive that help.

It may come in the form of a book, a certain speaker, or a friend who says just what you need to hear at the moment. Or it may come through a personal testimony or even a direct dealing from the Lord Himself. Today may be God's appointed time for you as you are reading *this* book. If so, it will be used by Him in some area in which you are hurting at the present. It may be the beginning of your recovery, the next step in that process, or even the finishing touch in your long struggle for wholeness.

Many people who come to me for prayer for emotional healing are concerned and even distraught because there are portions of their childhood that they cannot recall. They have been on what I call "digging expeditions," trying to unearth forgotten memories so they can face them, deal with them and get them out of their system. I always delight in telling such people that there are still portions of my own past that I can't recall. Actually, much of my childhood seems to be filled with blank pages.

I remind such people that the Holy Spirit leads us into all truth and is able to bring many things to our remembrance. But we must allow Him to do the leading in this sensitive area. I have put Him in charge of my memory. I truly believe that if remembering something from my past is going to help me, then I will recall it. If it will not help me, is unnecessary or would even be harmful for me to remember, then I am thankful that I can't recall it. I believe that sometimes what we don't know can't hurt us.

Obviously, this is not always the case. Many times people experience great relief by recalling some traumatic event, dealing with it and then getting on with their lives. Sometimes if memories have been shut out on purpose and "stuffed" deep within the recesses of the mind, they will poison the entire system. In that case, the memories must be exposed before wholeness can be established. Yet, here again, it is important to remember that if this process is not done with the leadership and guidance of the Holy Spirit, it can be harmful and actually cause even more damage to already wounded emotions.

The Holy Spirit is gentle, tender, considerate, kind, loving and patient. Yet, He is also powerful and mighty and able to do what man can never do on his own. The psalmist says, **Except the Lord builds the house, they labor in vain who build it; except the Lord keeps the city, the watchman wakes but in vain** (Ps. 127:1). I spent many years of my life waking and laboring in vain. I encourage you not to waste the most precious years of your life trying to "do it yourself." Seek God and His plan for your recovery. He will lead you one step at a time, and you will be transformed "from glory to glory." (2 Cor. 3:18 KJV.)

6
Pain

Even when the Holy Spirit is allowed to lead, emotional healing is still painful. If you will let the Spirit of the Lord direct your recovery program, He will always be there to provide the strength you need in each phase, so that whatever trials you may have to face, you will be able to bear them.

Even though the Lord has promised never to leave us nor forsake us (Heb. 13:5), when we get ahead of God and begin to "do our own thing," we are in dangerous territory. Our heavenly Father is under no obligation to sustain us in bearing trials that were never a part of His plan for us. We may well survive, but the process will involve much more struggle than was necessary.

The pain of emotional wounding and healing can be even more traumatic than physical pain. When you are following God's revealed plan, and you come to painful times, remember that the Holy Spirit is the Strengthener. Sometimes it may seem that you are not going to make it through. At such moments, ask the Lord to strengthen you.

A great Scripture to memorize for these difficult times is 1 Corinthians 10:13 in which the Apostle Paul reminds us that . . . **no temptation (no trial regarded as enticing to sin, no matter how it comes or where it leads) has overtaken you and laid hold on you that is not common to man [that is, no temptation or trial has come to you that is beyond human resistance and that is not adjusted and adapted and belonging to human experience, and such as man can bear]. But God is faithful [to His Word and to His** compassionate nature], and He [can be trusted] not to let you be tempted and tried and assayed beyond your ability and strength of resistance and power to endure, but with the temptation He will [always] also provide the way out (the means of escape to a landing place), that you may be capable and strong and powerful to bear up under it patiently.

With such hard times come many temptations. Among these is the temptation to give up and revert to old thoughts and ways, to become negative, depressed and angry with God because you do not understand why He does not seem to be providing the way out of all the pain you have had to bear in your life. Yet this passage of Scripture tells us that God will always intervene on our behalf and that His help will always arrive on time. Purpose in your heart to hold on and not let go!

Another helpful passage is found in 2 Corinthians 12:7-9 in which Paul refers to his own suffering because of what he calls "a thorn in the flesh" (KJV). It really does not matter what the thorn was. Whatever it was, three times Paul sought God to take it away. Yet the Lord's answer to him was, . . . **My grace (My favor and loving-kindness and mercy) is enough for you [sufficient against any danger and enables you to bear the trouble manfully]; for My strength and power are made perfect . . . in [your] weakness . . .** (v. 9).

We are not always delivered from our distress at the precise moment we call on the name of the Lord. Sometimes we must endure for a while, be patient and continue in faith. Thank God, during those times in which the Lord decides for whatever reason not to deliver us right away, He always gives us the grace and strength we need to press on toward eventual victory.

Do you ever wonder *why* God does not always deliver us from our bondage and problems immediately? The reason is because only the Lord knows everything that needs to be done in the lives of His children — and the perfect timing for it to be done.

From my own experience, I have learned to trust rather than to question. It is not wrong to ask God why, unless that questioning produces confusion, in which case it is much better simply to trust the Lord, knowing that He is never wrong — and that He is never late! Often we understand the why behind an event or situation only after it is all over and we can stand on the other side of it, looking back on it. There are many experiences in my life that I certainly did not understand while I was going though them. Now, however, I have come to understand something of their meaning and purpose.

Going through trials is painful. In my ministry, I often share with people that the book of Revelation says that the brethren overcame the devil . . . **by the blood of the Lamb, and by the word of their testimony** . . . (Rev. 12:11 KJV). We overcome by the blood of the Lamb and by the word of our testimony. A testimony of victory in any area of life is important. However, in order to have a positive testimony, it is necessary to have successfully overcome some hardship or opposition. The painful part is what we must go through while we are being tempted and tested; the glorious part comes after we have finished going through the trial and can then testify of the great victory and God's great faithfulness.

Doorways of Pain

Because I personally experienced so much emotional pain, as you may have done also, I grew weary of hurting. I was attempting to find healing by following the leadership of the Holy Spirit. Yet I could not honestly understand why the process had to be so painful. I felt that if I were to be able to continue enduring the pain, I had to have some answers from the Lord. I was actually improving, getting better, gaining a victory here and there, but it seemed that every time I made any progress, the Lord would bring me into a new phase of recovery that would always mean more pain and emotional upset.

The Doorways of Pain

As I prayed about my situation, God gave me a vision. In my heart, I saw a series of doorways — one after another. Each represented a traumatic event in my past life that had brought pain when it had occurred. The Lord showed me how that each time I went through one of the painful events or situations (being sexually abused at home, being ridiculed at school because I was overweight; being unable to have any close friends; being subjected to constant fear; being abandoned by my husband; being betrayed by a group of friends at church; and so on), it was like a new doorway of pain.

I can remember vividly the anguish of abuse, fear, rejection, abandonment and betrayal — and so can you if you were a victim of these things which place people into such bondage.

When I finally allowed the Lord to begin to work in my life, He revealed to me I had been hiding behind many such "doorways of pain." I was *deep* in bondage, taking refuge behind false personalities, pretense and facades. I was simply unable to understand how to free myself. When the Lord began to bring me out of that bondage, it hurt.

What I was led to understand is that when people begin to be led out of bondage and into freedom, they must pass back through the same, or similar, doorways of pain that they previously went through. The reason they must do so is to get on the other side of them. In order to deliver and to heal, the Lord must lead us to face issues, people and truths that we find difficult, if not impossible, to face on our own. Let me give you several examples.

Example One

I was always terrified of my father. Even as a grown woman in my forties, with four children of my own, I was still frightened of him. Many painful events had brought that fear into my life. The Lord led me to realize that I had to confront my father, look him straight in the eye and tell him, "*I am not afraid of you anymore.*" I did it in obedience and by faith, but not without "fear and trembling." (Phil. 2:12 KJV.) I had come face to face with one of the doorways of pain. I knew that either I could go back through it and come out free on the other side, or I could stay behind the door, hiding, and remain forever afraid of my own father.

Remember: *I confronted the primary cause of my pain because the Holy Spirit led me to do so; do not try this sort of thing just because I did it.*

Example Two

Sometimes people get hurt in the church by other Christians. Somehow we seem to think that believers should not hurt other believers — and they shouldn't. But things are seldom as they ought to be, even in the lives of

God's people. We in the Church do hurt one another and it does cause pain.

Frequently, when this happens, the injured party withdraws from any association or involvement with the ones who caused the pain. Hiding behind a doorway of pain, the wounded individual may decide: "Since I got hurt at church, I will continue to go to services (maybe), but I will never get involved with those people again." That is a form of bondage because the person is allowing the past to control him.

God will bring us to a place in which we must step out of hiding and take a chance on being hurt again. When we do step out, it is the equivalent of going back through the same doorway of pain that led us into bondage.

Example Three

Learning to submit to authority is very difficult for some people. It was extremely painful for me. Since I had been abused by every authority figure I had ever known, my attitude was, "Why should I allow someone else to tell me what to do?" I did not trust anyone, especially men.

When the Holy Spirit led me to the phase of my recovery in which I had to submit to my husband, the battle was on! I experienced a terrible sense of rebellion in my flesh. I wanted to be submissive, because I truly believed that it was scriptural, but the pain of submission was more then I knew how to handle.

I did not understand what was wrong with me. I realize now that submitting to someone else and allowing that person to make decisions for me brought back all the old fears and memories of being manipulated and taken advantage of. Having my father (an authority figure) trying to tell me that the hurtful decisions he was making for me were for my good, and all the time hating so much what he was doing to me, combined with my frustrations at being unable to do anything about it all, did not leave me thrilled about submission.

In order to be set free and to become the whole person that God desired for me to be, I had to learn to submit to my husband. Like many other Christians, I believed that the Scriptures teach that submission of the wife and children to the husband and father as the head of the home is God's revealed plan for families. I was convinced that this principle is set forth in His Word and that therefore I had no choice but to submit to it, or be in rebellion against the Lord. But it certainly was painful! Now, I am free and can see the safety and security in *godly* submission.

Note: Many people get confused about submission. They think that it means that they must do everything an authority tells them to do, no matter what it is. The Bible teaches that we should be submissive only . . . **as it is fit in the Lord** (Col. 3:18 KJV).

I trust that these examples will help you understand the "doorways of pain" and how they must be faced. Don't look upon them as the entrance to suffering but as the threshold of recovery. Jesus will always be with you to lead you and strengthen you as you pass through these gateways to wholeness.

Remember: *Pain is really a part of the healing process.*

Another example the Lord gave me is that of a skinned knee. If a person falls on concrete and skins his knee badly, he will most definitely hurt. The next day, the pain may be even worse than when the wound was fresh. By that time a scab may have begun to form, which is a sign that his body is involved in the process of healing. But although now covered with the protective scab, his wound is also drawing, burning and throbbing because of the increase of blood rushing to bring healing to the affected area.

Think about it: A wound brings pain, but often healing brings even worse pain. Yet they are not the same kind of pain, nor do they have the same result. Some people's emotional wounds have been ignored for so long they have become infected. That kind of pain is totally different from the pain of healing. One is to be avoided; the other is to be welcomed.

No Pain, No Gain!

Let me share with you an excellent piece of wisdom that I learned through personal experience: *Don't be afraid of pain!* As strange as it may seem, the more you dread and resist it, the more you increase its effect upon you.

Years ago I went on a fast for the first time in my life. God called me to a twenty-eight-day juice fast. In the beginning, I went through some really hard times. I was very, very hungry. In fact, I was so famished that I was in actual pain. As I cried out to the Lord, complaining that I just could not stand it any longer, He answered me. Deep within me I heard the "still, small voice" (1 Kings 19:12 KJV) of the Lord say to me, "*Stop fighting the pain; let it do its work.*" From that time on, the fast was much easier, even enjoyable, because I knew that every time I felt discomfort it was a sign of progress.

The rule is that the more pain is resisted, the stronger it becomes. When a pregnant woman begins to go into labor, the advice she is given by her attendants is "*Relax.*" They know that the more she fights the pain, the stronger it will become, and the longer the delivery process will take.

When you are going through a difficult time, when the pain becomes so severe that it seems to be more than you can endure, remember Hebrews 12:2: **Looking away [from all that will distract] to Jesus, Who is the Leader and the Source of our faith [giving the first incentive for our belief] and is also its Finisher [bringing it to maturity and** perfection]. He, for the joy [of obtaining the prize] that was set before Him, endured the cross, despising and ignoring the shame, and is now seated at the right hand of the throne of God.

Endurance Produces Joy

They who sow in tears shall reap in joy and singing.
Psalm 126:5

When you are experiencing pain, don't fight it. Allow it to accomplish its purpose.

Learn to endure whatever you need to, knowing that there is joy on the other side!

Why not? You are hurting anyway; you may as well reap the full benefit of your suffering. As long as you allow past abuse to keep you in bondage, you will live in continual pain. At least the pain of healing produces a positive result — joy instead of misery.

Let your pain lead you out of bondage, not deeper into it. Do the right thing, even if it is hard. Obey God and follow the leading of the Holy Spirit knowing that . . .**Weeping may endure for a night, but joy comes in the morning** (Ps. 30:5).

7
The Only Way Out Is Through

In one of our meetings, a woman came forward asking for a certain bondage to be broken in her life. As soon as I started to pray for her, she began to cry. Almost immediately I received a vision of her standing on a track, as though she were about to run a race. As I watched, I saw that every time the race would begin, and she would start moving toward the finish line, she would go about halfway and then turn around and come back to the starting line.

After a while, she would repeat the process. This happened time after time. I shared with her what I was seeing and told her that I believed that God was saying to her, "This time, you need to go *all the way through*." As I shared that message with her, she immediately bore witness, agreeing that God was speaking to her. Her problem was that although she often made some progress toward emotional healing, she always gave up under pressure. Now she was determined to see the process through to complete victory.

Remember this: *It is always much harder to finish than it is to start.*

There really are no "quick-fix" methods to emotional healing. In 2 Corinthians 3:18 the Apostle Paul speaks of Christians being transformed "from one degree of glory to another." If you are going through the difficult process of emotional healing, I encourage you to enjoy the degree of "glory" you are currently experiencing as you move toward the next level.

Many people turn emotional healing or recovery from abuse into such an ordeal that they never allow themselves to enjoy any aspect of it. Do not allow yourself to be tempted to focus on how far you have to go. Instead look at how far you have come! Adopt this as your attitude:

I am not where I need to be,

but, thank God, I am not where I used to be.

I'm okay, and I'm on my way!

Remember: *You have a life to live while you are being healed!*

Going Through

In some aspects, spiritual growth can be compared to physical growth. I think it would be safe to say that many people do not enjoy their children while they are raising them. At each stage of growth, the parents wish the child was in another stage. If the child is crawling, they wish he were walking, out of diapers, in school, graduating, getting married, giving them grandchildren, and on and on.

We should learn to enjoy each stage of life as it comes because each has joys and trials uniquely its own. As Christians, we are growing throughout our lifetime. We never stop progressing. Make a decision right now to begin to enjoy yourself while you are striving to reach each new level of victory.

In Deuteronomy 7:22, Moses told the children of Israel that the Lord would drive out their enemies before them "little by little." Between each victory in our lives, there is a time of waiting. During this time the Holy Spirit deals with us, opening to us new revelations, helping us to face and receive even greater truths. The waiting is usually difficult for most of us because impatience is always present within us to stir up dissatisfaction. We want everything *now*!

Patience Reaps Promises

Do not, therefore, fling away your fearless confidence, for it carries a great and glorious compensation of reward.

For you have need of steadfast patience and endurance, so that you may perform and fully accomplish the will of God, and thus receive and carry away [and enjoy to the full] what is promised.

For still a little while (a very little while), and the Coming One will come and He will not delay.

Hebrews 10:35-37

From this passage we see that we need faith, patience and endurance in order to receive the end result of fulfilled promises.

In Hebrews 6:11 we read: **But we do [strongly and earnestly] desire for each of you to show the same diligence and sincerity [*all the way through*] in realizing and enjoying the full assurance and development of [your] hope until the end.**

You can see that in order to get *out*, we must go *through*.

In Isaiah 43:1,2, the Lord admonishes His people,

. . . Fear not . . . I have called you by your name; you are Mine.

When you *pass through* the waters, I will be with you, and *through* the rivers, they will not overwhelm you. When you *walk through* the fire, you will not be burned or scorched, nor will the flame kindle upon you.

In Psalm 23:4, David said of the Lord, . . . **though I *walk through* the [deep, sunless] valley of the shadow of death, I will fear or dread no evil, for You are with me; Your rod [to protect] and Your staff [to guide], they comfort me.**

Often a person who is rooted in abuse ends up with strongholds in his mind and flesh that must be allowed to pass through the valley of the shadow of death if they are ever to be pulled down and destroyed. (2 Cor. 10:4.)

For example, as a result of having been abused for so long, I developed a very independent personality. I did not trust anyone. Early in life I came to the conclusion that if I took care of myself and never asked anyone for anything, then I would get hurt less. As the Lord began to reveal to me that my independent attitude was not scriptural, I had to "walk it through the valley of the shadow of death." In other words, I had to let that old nature (part of the old Joyce) go to the cross and die.

The temptation is to run away from our problems, but the Lord says that we are to *go through* them. The good news is that He has promised that we will never have to go through them alone. He will always be there to help us in every way. He has said to us, "Fear not, for I am with you."

When we begin our journey to wholeness with the Lord, we are usually all knotted up inside. As we allow Him to do so, He begins to straighten up our lives by untying "one knot at a time."

To some of His first disciples Jesus said, "I am the way, follow Me." When you decide to follow Jesus, you will soon learn that He never turns back in fear. His path is always straightforward to the finish line. Do not be like the woman in my prayer line who always gave up halfway through the race. As difficult as it may be, decide to stay in the race and see it *through!*

8
Guilt and Shame

Shame is not to be confused with guilt and condemnation. Guilt is a huge problem in our society today because most people experience plenty of it. The devil wants all of us to feel *wrong* about ourselves. Jesus Christ gave His life that we might have righteousness — or as I like to write it, *RIGHT*eousness.

We were created by God to feel right and good about ourselves. However, because of the presence of sin in the world, and the sin nature that came upon us through the fall of mankind, we cannot now *do* everything right. When we accept Jesus as our Savior, He imparts or gives to us the gift of righteousness. By faith, we are made *right* with God.

In 2 Corinthians 5:21 the Apostle Paul tells us what God did for us: **For our sake He made Christ [virtually] to be sin Who knew no sin, so that in and through Him we might become [endued with, viewed as being in, and examples of] the righteousness of God [what we ought to be, approved and acceptable and in right relationship with Him, by His goodness].**

God sent Jesus to redeem us (that is, to buy us back from the devil to whom we had sold ourselves as slaves to sin), to restore us (to make us as we were supposed to be in the beginning). We were created — and redeemed — by God for righteousness, not shame, guilt and condemnation.

No Condemnation in Christ

Therefore, [there is] *now* no condemnation (no adjudging guilty of wrong) for those who are in Christ

Jesus, who live [and] walk not after the dictates of the flesh, but after the dictates of the Spirit.

Romans 8:1

Of course, if we would follow the leading of the Holy Spirit, we would never do anything wrong, so guilt would have no place to take root. However, since we are human, none of us is incapable of making a mistake. As our Lord pointed out in Matthew 26:41 (KJV), . . . **the spirit indeed is willing, but the flesh is weak.**

How then can we live free from guilt if we cannot perform perfectly even though we would like to? By walking in the Spirit. We sin when we get out of the Spirit. Condemnation and guilt feelings come as a result of sin. The devil sees an opening and immediately moves to take advantage of it. The moment of temptation is a crucial point to deal with if we ever hope to be able to live without guilt.

Once you have given into temptation or fallen into sin, instead of trying to restore yourself through good works, which is walking after the flesh, choose to turn back to the Spirit. (You sinned in the first place because you got out of the Spirit.) If you keep following the flesh, you will only get deeper and deeper into trouble and turmoil. Instead, turn back to following the Spirit, allowing Him to lead and guide you in correcting your situation. The Spirit always has the correct answer for every problem.

For example, the Spirit will lead to repentance, which produces forgiveness from God: **If we [freely] admit that we have sinned and confess our sins, He is faithful and just (true to His own nature and promises) and will forgive our sins [dismiss our lawlessness] and [continuously] cleanse us from all unrighteousness [everything not in conformity to His will in purpose, thought, and action]** (1 John 1:9).

The flesh will lead to works that supposedly win the right to receive God's favor. The flesh always attempts to repay for mistakes rather than simply receiving God's gift of pardon and restoration.

Dealing With Guilt

The Lord once gave me a great revelation about guilt.

I had felt guilty as long as I could remember. Guilt was my constant companion. We went everywhere together! It began early in my childhood when I was being sexually abused. Even though my father told me that what he was doing to me was not wrong, it made me feel dirty and guilty. Of course, as I got older and became aware that it was wrong, but had no way to make it stop, the guilt continued and increased.

What is guilt? How does it feel? Guilt is a heaviness, an unbearable burden that depresses the spirit. Jesus is our glory and the *lifter* of our heads. (Ps. 3:3.) Satan is the accuser (Rev. 12:10); He wants to press us down. Guilt makes everything seem dark and heavy. It makes us feel tired and weary. Actually it draws our energy and saps the strength we need to resist sin and Satan. So the result is that guilt and condemnation actually increase sin.

I believe that I was addicted to guilt. I can never remember being guilt-free! Even if I wasn't doing anything particularly bad or sinful, I found something to feel *wrong* about.

For example, I was shopping one day, with my ever-present companion of guilt with me. I do not recall what I had done wrong this time; it doesn't even matter, it was always something. I was about to get out of my car and go into a store when the Holy Spirit said to me, "Joyce, how do you plan to get forgiveness for this sin?" I knew the right answer. I said, "I'll accept the sacrifice Jesus made for me when He died at Calvary." We can know the right answer (have head knowledge), and still not be applying it to our own situation.

Then the Holy Spirit continued: "I see, Joyce, and *when* do you plan to accept Jesus' sacrifice?" A major revelation began to shine forth in me! At that moment I knew that I could wait two or three days until I *felt* guilty long enough and then accept God's forgiveness, or I could receive that pardon right then.

I always asked for forgiveness for my sins right away, but I never accepted it until I *felt* that I had suffered enough to pay for it. God caused me to realize what I was doing, how much unnecessary pain I was causing myself. He even showed me that what I was doing was insulting to Jesus, that in essence I was saying, "Lord, the sacrifice of Your life and blood was good, but not good enough. I must add my work of guilty feelings before I can be forgiven."

That very day I began getting free from guilt and condemnation. I encourage you to do the same. Remember: Guilt does no good at all! It accomplishes nothing, except the following:

1. Guilt drains your energy and can even make you physically or mentally ill.

2. Guilt blocks fellowship with God. Hebrews 4:15,16 says, **For we do not have a High Priest Who is unable to understand and sympathize and have a shared feeling with our weaknesses and infirmities and liability to the assaults of temptation, but One Who has been tempted in every respect as we are, yet without sinning. Let us then fearlessly and confidently and *boldly* draw near to the throne of grace (the throne of God's unmerited favor to us sinners), that we may receive mercy [for our failures] and find grace to help in good time for every need [appropriate help and well-timed help, coming just when we need it].**

3. Guilt, as a work of the flesh, declares that you are trying to pay for your sin.

4. Guilt drains your spiritual energy. It leaves you weak and unable to resist new attacks from the enemy. Successful

spiritual warfare requires wearing of the "breastplate of RIGHTeousness." (Eph. 6:14 KJV.) Guilt causes you to sin more.

5. Guilt exerts such tremendous pressure on you that getting along with others is difficult. It is nearly impossible to live under a burden of guilt and still operate in the fruit of the Spirit. (Gal. 5:22,23.)

Surely you can see from this list that guilt is a good thing to give up. Let it go! It is from the devil and is intended to prevent you from ever enjoying your life or your relationship with the Lord.

If you have a big problem in this area of guilt, you may need to ask someone to pray for you. If your faith is strong enough, pray for yourself. However, guilt robs faith; if you have lived for a long time buried under a load of guilt and condemnation, your faith may need to be strengthened. Get the help you need. Refuse to live any longer pressed down under a burden of guilt and condemnation.*

What About Shame?

Now that we have a better understanding of guilt, let's turn our attention to the subject of shame.

There is a shame that is normal and healthy. If I lose or break something that belongs to someone else, I feel ashamed of my mistake. I wish I had not been so careless or negligent. I am sorry, but I can ask for forgiveness, receive it, and then go on with my life. Healthy shame reminds us that we are human beings with weaknesses and limitations.

What does Genesis 2:25 mean when it says that, in the Garden of Eden, Adam and Eve were naked and were not

---

*To purchase a four-tape cassette series on guilt and condemnation, write me for a tape catalog.

ashamed? Besides the fact that they were not wearing any clothes, I believe it means that they were totally open and honest with each other, hiding behind no masks, playing no games. They were completely free to be themselves because they had no sense of shame. Once they had sinned, however, they went and hid themselves. (Gen. 3:6-8.)

People should be able to enjoy perfect freedom with each other and with God, but very few are able to do so. Most people pretend. They produce false personalities and hide behind them. They act as if they are not hurt when they are, or they pretend that they don't need anyone when they do.

There is a *poisonous shame* that can drastically affect the quality of a person's life. This occurs when an individual who is being abused or mistreated in some way begins to internalize the shame he feels. He is no longer just ashamed of what is being done to him, but he becomes *ashamed of himself* because of what he is being subjected to.

Such an individual takes the shame into himself where it actually becomes the core of his being. Everything in his life becomes poisoned by his emotions so that he develops into a shame-based person.

At one time I was shame-based, but I didn't know I was ashamed of myself. I was seeing the results of shame in my life, but was unsuccessfully trying to deal with the fruit rather than the root.

The definition of the word translated "ashamed" in the *King James Version* of Genesis 2:25 is: ". . . (by. impl.) to *be disappointed*, or *delayed* . . . confounded."[1]

This word "confounded" simply means to be frustrated or confused. *Webster's New World Dictionary* defines the

---

[1]James Strong, *Strong's Exhaustive Concordance of the Bible* (Nashville: Abingdon, 1978), "Hebrew and Chaldee Dictionary," p. 19, entry # 954.

verb "confound" as: ". . . confuse"; "bewilder"; "damn."[2]
Webster defines the verb "damn" as: "to condemn to an
unhappy fate"; "doom"; "to criticize adversely"; "to cause
the ruin of"; "make fail."[3]

If you will take the time to really study these definitions,
you may discover that the root of your problem is shame.

Dealing With Shame

Let me explain something about shame from my own
experience.

My life was filled with confusion because I was trying
desperately to do right (so I could "feel right"), but no
matter how hard I tried, I always failed. It seemed as if I
were *doomed* to failure. I didn't fail at everything, however. I
was successful in the corporate world, and in a few other
areas, but I was a failure at godly behavior. I always felt
defeated because no matter what I accomplished on the
outside, I still felt bad about myself on the inside.

I was ashamed of me!

I didn't like who I was. I didn't like my basic personality.
I was continually rejecting my real self and trying to be
someone or something I was not and never could be. (I will
discuss this topic more fully in another chapter.)

Multiplied thousands of Christians spend their entire
lives in this pitiful condition — living far, far below their
rightful position as heirs of God and joint-heirs with Jesus
Christ. (Rom. 8:17 KJV.) I know, because I was one of them.

It was a great day when the Holy Spirit led me to
understand that shame was the source of many of my
problems! There are promises in the Word of God that

---

[2]*Webster's New World Dictionary*, 3d college ed. s.v. "confound."
[3]*Ibid*. s.v. "damn."

assure us that we can be delivered from a sense of shame. For example, there is Isaiah 61:7:

Instead of your [former] shame you shall have a twofold recompense; instead of dishonor and reproach [your people] shall rejoice in their portion. Therefore in their land they shall possess double [what they had forfeited]; everlasting joy shall be theirs.

Wow! Let's examine this passage which offers "a twofold recompense." A recompense is a reward or compensation for injury. In other words, if you trust God and do things His way, He will see to it that you are repaid for every injustice ever done to you. You will receive double what you have forfeited or lost, and everlasting joy will be yours! That is a wonderful promise, and I can vouch for the reality of it. God has done that very thing for me, and He will do it for you too.

Another promise from the Lord is found in Isaiah 54:4:

Fear not, for you shall not be ashamed; neither be confounded and depressed, for you shall not be put to shame. For you shall forget the shame of your youth, and you shall not [seriously] remember the reproach of your widowhood any more.

Wow! Double wow! How inspiring and encouraging it is to know that you will forget the harm of your past and will never have to *seriously* remember those hard, hard times!

There is even a promise that you can stand on if you are still being abused or mistreated. Perhaps you feel that the Lord has told you to endure for a season some verbal or emotional abuse while He is doing a work in the person who is hurting you. How can you protect yourself from developing a shame-based nature? The prayer of the psalmist can be yours also: **O keep me, Lord, and deliver me; let me not be ashamed or disappointed, for my trust and my refuge are in You** (Ps. 25:20).

God can keep you from shame. I suggest that every time you suffer from verbal or emotional abuse, simply pray and ask God to keep you from the shame that tries to build up within you. Use this word in Psalm 25:20 as a double-edged sword against the enemy (which in this case is shame).

Following is an example of how this approach will work for your benefit.

I know a pastor's wife who has no problems at all in her sexual relations with her husband, even though she was sexually abused by relatives for many years. On the other hand, as a result of my sexual abuse, I had many, many problems to confront and overcome in my sexual relations with my husband.

What made the difference? While questioning my friend, I discovered that throughout her childhood she had maintained a strong faith in God. The abuse began when she was about fourteen years of age. By that time she had already enjoyed many years of good Christian fellowship and an active prayer life. She prayed each time her abusers molested her, asking God to cover her so it would not affect her sexual relationship with her future husband. She knew that one day she was going to marry a pastor because the Lord had already revealed it to her. Her prayers protected her from shame and bondage in that area.

In my case, I did not know enough about God to activate my faith through prayer. Therefore I did suffer from shame — until I discovered that I was shame-based and learned about God's promises to deliver me. You can also be delivered from shame, which is the source of many complex inner problems, such as:

Alienation

Compulsive behaviors (drug / alcohol / substance abuse; eating disorders; addiction to money, work, or other objects or activities; sexual perversions; excessive need to be in control; lack of self-control or self-discipline; gossiping; judgmental spirit; etc.)

Depression

Deep sense of inferiority ("There-is-something-wrong-with-me" thinking)

Failure syndrome

Isolating loneliness

Lack of confidence

Neurotic behavior (a neurotic assumes too much responsibility; in times of conflict he automatically presumes that he is at fault)

Perfectionism

Timidity (fear of all types)

Depression

For as he thinks in his heart, so is he. . . .
Proverbs 23:7

In conclusion, let me offer a word about depression. Extreme numbers of people suffer from this terrible condition, which has many complex causes, one of which is shame. If you are prone to depression, it may be a sign of a deeper problem, a root of shame.

Those who are shame-based think and speak negatively about themselves. Such wrong thinking and speaking places a heavy weight on the spirit. This is a major problem because human beings were created by God for righteousness, love and acceptance. God is always pouring forth these things upon His children, but many of His children do not know how to receive them.

You cannot receive these things from God if you are against yourself. If you have a problem in this area, don't just sit by and allow the devil to destroy you. Confront your spiritual enemy with spiritual action. Change your thinking and your speaking. Begin *purposely* to think and say only good things about yourself. Make a list of what the Word says about you and of your best qualities and confess it several times a day. Things like: I am the righteousness of God in Christ (2 Cor. 5:21). God loves me (John 3:16). I have gifts and abilities given to me by the Lord (Rom. 12:6-8). I am precious and valuable (Is. 43:4), etc., etc.

Another wise practice is to get a thorough medical examination to rule out the possibility of any physical condition that might be affecting your mental and emotional outlook. Unless your depression is caused by some health problem, it can usually be traced to negative thinking and speaking. Even when the depression is caused by some physical condition (hormonal or chemical imbalance, etc.), the devil will take advantage of the situation. He will offer many negative thoughts which, if received and meditated upon, will only make the problem seem many times worse than it actually is.

I repeat: *When you feel depressed, check your thinking. It is not God's will for you to be depressed.*

Isaiah 61:3 says that the Lord has given us . . . **the garment [expressive] of praise instead of a heavy, burdened, and failing spirit** . . . .

According to Psalm 3:3 He is a shield for us, our glory, and the lifter of our heads.

 . . . **The joy of the Lord is your strength and stronghold** (Neh. 8:10).

Believe what the Word says you are, and that is what you will become. Believe what the devil says you are, and you will become that. The choice is yours: . . . **therefore choose life, that you and your descendants may live** (Deut. 30:19).

9
Self-Rejection and Self-Hatred

Shame causes self-rejection and, in some cases, even self-hatred. In more extreme cases, it can develop into self-abuse, including self-mutilation. I have ministered to several people who have shown me scars on their bodies from their cutting, burning or biting themselves, as well as bruises from their beating or hitting themselves and bald spots from their pulling out their own hair.

Some people even starve themselves as a form of self-punishment. Others behave in an obnoxious manner so that they will be rejected. Since they have rejected themselves, they are convinced they will be rejected by others, so they manifest behavior in accordance with what they believe about themselves. The list of potential problems goes on and on, but I am sure you see the point I am making:

You cannot get beyond your own opinion of yourself — no matter how many good things God may say about you in His Word. Regardless of all the wonderful plans God may have for your life, none of them will come to pass without your cooperation.

You need to believe what God says.

God's Opinion of You
and His Will for You

If you are seeking recovery from abuse, you must not allow other people's opinions of you, as evidenced by the way you have been mistreated in the past, to determine your worth. Remember, people who feel worthless will always try to find something wrong with you so they can feel a little better about themselves. Keep in mind that this is their problem, not yours.

In John 3:18 the Lord Jesus states that no one who believes in Him will *ever* be rejected by Him or His heavenly Father. If God accepts you because of your faith in His Son Jesus Christ, then you can decide to stop rejecting yourself so that your healing process can continue.

It may be that you are not totally rejecting yourself, but only parts of yourself that are displeasing to you. In my own case, I rejected my personality. I did not understand that I had a divine calling on my life to full-time ministry and that my basic temperament was designed by God for what He had for me to do. My personality was flawed, of course, due to the years of abuse I had suffered, and was in need of Holy Spirit adjustment, but it was still the basic personality that God had chosen for me. However, because I did not understand that fact, I thought I had to become totally different. I was constantly trying to be someone else, which was not God's will for me — nor is it His will that you become someone else.

Remember: God will help you be all *you* can be — all you were originally designed to be. But He will never permit you to be successful at becoming someone else.

The Spirit-Controlled Temperament

Did you ever find yourself thinking this way about another person, a friend or perhaps a spiritual leader: "He is the way people *ought* to be," or "She is liked and accepted *by everyone*"? Perhaps without even consciously planning it, you started trying to be like that individual.

Of course, other people can be good examples to us, but even if we pattern ourselves after their good qualities, it must still be our own personal "flavor" of those good traits that characterizes us.

I have a bold, straightforward, decisive, take-charge personality. God instilled that type of nature in me to help me fulfill His call upon my life. However, for many, many years I struggled and lived in frustration because I kept trying to be more timid, mild, gentle, quiet and sweet. I tried desperately not to be so assertive and aggressive.

The truth is that I vainly tried to model myself after my pastor's wife, my husband and various friends whom I respected and admired. My efforts only resulted in increased frustration, which made me even more difficult to get along with. What I needed to learn to do was to quit trying to be like others and simply become "the best *me* I could be." Yes, I did need change. I did need more of the fruit of the Spirit — especially kindness, gentleness and meekness — because I was too hard, harsh and abrasive. But once I learned to accept my basic, God-given temperament, then I was able to let the Holy Spirit begin to change me into what He wanted me to be.

Once I quit my striving, then the Spirit was able to use my strengths and to control my weaknesses. I began to develop a "Spirit-controlled temperament."

Many years have passed since I finally learned that I had to accept and love myself, not hate and reject myself. I have since discovered the secret of the Spirit-controlled temperament. The key is spending quality personal time with the Lord and receiving help from Him on a regular basis.

Strengthened in the Inner Man

[I pray God] **That he would grant you, according to the riches of his glory, to be strengthened with might by his Spirit in the inner man;**

That Christ may dwell in your hearts by faith . . . and . . . [that you may be] rooted and grounded in love.

Ephesians 3:16,17 KJV

I still have weaknesses in my natural man; however, as long as I abide in the Lord, seeking Him first, He continually imparts to me the power I need to manifest my strengths and not my weaknesses.

In Ephesians 3:16,17 the Apostle Paul prayed that the believers in Ephesus would be strengthened "in the inner man," that the Holy Spirit would indwell their innermost being and personality. This is our great need. God told Paul that His strength is made perfect in weakness. (2 Cor. 12:9 KJV.) When we are weak in a certain area, we do not have to hate or reject ourselves because of it. Like Paul, we have the great privilege of admitting our weaknesses and asking the Holy Spirit to control them.

In my flesh, I still have a tendency to be sharp, rude and blunt. By the grace, strength and power of the Lord, however, I am able to manifest "the fruit of the Spirit" (Gal. 5:22,23) and to be kind, pleasant, understanding and longsuffering.

That doesn't mean that I never fail. Like everyone else, I slip and make mistakes. But I have come to understand that I don't have to be perfect in order to receive acceptance, love and help from the Lord. Neither do you.

God is *for* you! He wants *you* to be for *you*. The devil is *against* you, and he wants *you* to be against *you*.

Are you for yourself or against yourself? Are you cooperating with God's plan for your life, or with the devil's plan for you? Are you in agreement with God or with the enemy?

Accepted in the Beloved

According as he [God] hath chosen us in him [Christ] before the foundation of the world, that we should be holy and without blame before him in love ....

To the praise of the glory of his grace, wherein he hath made us accepted in the beloved.

Ephesians 1:4,6 KJV

In Exodus 19:5 the Lord tells His people that they are His own "peculiar possession and treasure." That word applies to us today as much as it did to the children of Israel. In John 3:18 Jesus told Nicodemus that no one who believes in Him will ever be condemned (rejected). You may not feel treasured or even acceptable, but you are. In Ephesians 1:6 Paul says that all of us who believe in Christ have been "accepted in the beloved." That should give us a sense of personal value and worth.

I remember standing in a prayer line where I overheard a woman next to me telling the pastor who was ministering to her how much she hated and despised herself. The pastor became very firm with her and in a strong manner rebuked her, saying, "Who do you think you are? You have no right to hate yourself. God paid a high price for you and your freedom. He loved you so much that He sent His only Son to die for you . . . to suffer in your place. You have no right to hate or reject yourself. Your part is to receive what Jesus died to give you!"

The woman was shocked. I was shocked, too, just listening. Yet sometimes it takes a strong word to get us to realize the trap that Satan has set for us.

Self-rejection and self-hatred can almost seem pious in a sense. They can become a way of punishing ourselves for our mistakes, failures and inabilities. We cannot be perfect, so we reject and despise ourselves.

I ask you to think of these prophetic words in Isaiah 53:3 which describe our Lord Jesus Christ: **He was despised and rejected and forsaken by men, a Man of sorrows and pains, and acquainted with grief and sickness; and like One from Whom men hide their faces He was despised, and we did not appreciate His worth or have any esteem for Him.**

Do you lack appreciation for your own worth and value? Surely, you are valuable; otherwise your heavenly

Father would not have paid such a heavy price for your redemption.

Isaiah 53:4,5 goes on to say that Christ . . . **has borne our griefs (sicknesses, weaknesses, and distresses) . . . He was wounded for our transgressions, He was bruised for our guilt and iniquities; the chastisement [needful to obtain] peace and well-being for us was upon Him, and with the stripes [that wounded] Him we are healed and made whole.**

The "healing package" purchased by Jesus with His blood is available to all who will believe and receive. That package includes the healing of the emotions as well as the body. If a person has done wrong, justice demands rejection, despising and condemnation. However, Jesus bore all that for us, just as He bore our sins. What a glorious truth!

Since Jesus bore your sins on the cross, along with the hatred, rejection and condemnation they deserved, you don't have to reject or hate yourself anymore.

Do this: Wrap your arms around yourself and give yourself a big hug. Say: "I no longer reject myself! Instead, I accept myself in Christ. I love myself. I am not perfect, but with the help of the Lord I am improving day by day."

What About Rejection From Others?

And Jesus increased in wisdom and stature, and in favour with God and man.
                                Luke 2:52 KJV

Most likely sooner or later you will experience some form of rejection. Not everybody will like you. Some people may even aggressively dislike you. It is extremely helpful that you develop a mature attitude in this area. In my own case, I ask God for favor with Him and with people, and I believe that He provides it. I suggest that you do the same. Here is a prayer to help you achieve an acceptable attitude:

Today, Lord, I am going to do my best, with Your help, and for Your glory. I realize that there are many different people in the world with a variety of opinions and expectations. I probably won't please all of them all of the time. I will concentrate on being a God-pleaser and not a self-pleaser or a man-pleaser. The rest I leave in Your hands, Lord. Grant me favor with You and with men, and continue transforming me into the image of Your dear Son. Thank You, Lord.

No one enjoys being rejected, but all of us can learn to handle rejection and get on with our lives, if we remember that Jesus was also rejected and despised. He gained the victory over rejection by being faithful to God's plan for His life.

Rejection from other people wounds our emotions. It certainly hurts, and yet, for our own sake, we must remember that, if we are born again, the Helper (the Holy Spirit) lives in us to strengthen, undergird and comfort us.

I think we spend valuable time and energy trying to avoid being rejected. We become "menpleasers." (Eph. 6:6; Col. 3:22 KJV.) After all, we reason, if we can keep everyone else happy, they won't reject us. To avoid pain, we build walls around ourselves so we won't get hurt. That is pointless. God has shown me that it is impossible to live in this world if we are not willing to get hurt.

I have a wonderful husband, but occasionally he does hurt me. Because I come from such a painful background, the moment that kind of thing happens, I usually throw up walls to protect myself. After all, no one can hurt me if I don't let anyone get close to me. However, I have learned that if I wall others out, I also wall myself in. If we build walls around ourselves out of fear, then we must tear them down out of faith.

The Lord has shown me that He wants to be my Protector, but He cannot do that if I am busy trying to protect myself. He has not promised that I will *never* get hurt, but He has promised to heal me if I come to Him rather than try to take care of everything myself.

People are not perfect, therefore we hurt and disappoint each other. Go to Jesus with each old wound, and begin to receive His healing grace. When someone hurts you, take that new wound to Jesus. Don't let it fester. Take it to the Lord and be willing to handle it His way and not your own.

Receive this Scripture as a personal promise from the Lord to you: **For I will restore health to you, and I will heal your wounds, says the Lord, because they have called you an outcast, saying, This is Zion, whom no one seeks after and for whom no one cares!** (Jer. 30:17).

Confess with the psalmist: **Although my father and my mother have forsaken me, yet the Lord will take me up [adopt me as His child]** (Ps. 27:10).

With the help of the Lord, you can survive rejection and find your completion "in Him."

10

The Root of Rejection and Its Effect on Relationships

A person who has a root of rejection in his life is usually handicapped in relationships.

In order to sustain healthy, loving, lasting relationships, a person must not fear rejection. When this fear becomes the motivating factor in the life of an individual, he will spend his time trying to avoid it rather than building healthy relationships.

Nobody goes through life totally escaping being rejected. Everyone experiences some rejection. However, if there has been enough of it to leave scars, it may cause the individual not only to function abnormally in his relationships with others, but also in his relationship with God. He may come to believe that he is loved *conditionally*. Feeling that he must earn the love of others, he may devote his life to trying to please them. He may fear that if he doesn't please them, they will withdraw their love from him, reject him or even abandon him.

Memory of the pain of such experiences often prevents personal liberty in relationships. People who have a fear of rejection, and the resulting loneliness and abandonment, usually end up allowing themselves to be controlled and manipulated by others. Since they believe that acceptance is based on performance, they are consumed with *doing* rather than *being*. Because they are afraid of simply being themselves, they spend their lives pretending — pretending to like people they detest, pretending they enjoy going places and doing things they hate, pretending that everything is fine when it isn't. Such people live in continual misery because they are afraid to be honest, to confront the real issues of life.

Pretending! Pretending! Pretending!

Since such people do not believe that they are lovable in themselves, often they will use the world's standards (money, status, clothes, natural talents, etc.) to prove to themselves and others that they are valuable. They live a life of misery, always trying to prove that they have worth and value.

No matter how much outward success a person may enjoy, he is not truly successful unless he knows who he is in Christ. Philippians 3:3 exhorts us to . . . **exult and glory and pride ourselves in Jesus Christ, and put no confidence or dependence [on what we are] in the flesh and on outward privileges and physical advantages and external appearances.**

It is important to remember that appearance is only the way we look, not the way we really are.

A person who is rejection-based is unable to receive love even when it is being freely offered to him. If he is able to accept love at all, it is only when he believes that he has earned it by behaving perfectly.

I remember a woman who once worked for my husband and me. She had grown up in an atmosphere of performance-based acceptance. When she did well in school, her father showed her love; when she did not do as well as he expected, he withheld his love from her. He behaved this way not only with his daughter but with other family members as well; therefore she learned that love was given as a reward for perfect performance and withheld as punishment for mistakes.

Like most people, she grew up not even realizing that her feelings and belief systems were in error. She assumed that all relationships were handled in this same way. Since she was an employee of our ministry, Life In The Word, there were occasions when I would ask her how her work was progressing, if she had everything caught up or if there was any job that she had been given that she was unable to get finished.

I began to notice that whenever I inquired about anything that this woman had not yet completed, she would begin to act very strangely. She would withdraw from me, avoid talking with me, and appear to work at a frenzied pace — all of which made me feel uncomfortable. Actually, I felt *rejected.*

I knew that as her employer I was entitled to the privilege of asking about her workload without having to go through a traumatic ordeal each time. So I finally confronted her about the situation, which only caused our relationship to become more strained and confused. It was obvious that neither of us really understood the root of the problem.

This was a woman who truly loved the Lord. She was intensely serious about her relationship with Him, so the situation provoked her to pray and ask God for some answers about her behavior. Too often we blame our bad behavior on someone else instead of seeking the Lord to get to the root of the problem so we can be set free.

The woman received a revelation from God that changed her entire life. The Lord showed her that because her father had rejected her when she did not perform perfectly, she mistakenly believed that everyone else was the same way. If any of her work was not fully completed by the time I inquired about it, she was convinced that I was rejecting her; therefore she withdrew from me. *I had not stopped loving her, but she had stopped receiving my love,* and so I too ended up feeling rejected.

We often do this same thing with the Lord. His love for us is not based on anything we do or do not do. In Romans 5:8, Paul tells us that God loved us when we were still in sin; that is, when we did not know Him at all — or even care. God's love is *always* flowing to all who will receive it. But like this employee who could not receive my love, often we reject God's love when we feel that we don't deserve it because our performance is less than perfect.

Fear of Being Rejected
Causes Rejection of Others

If you cannot believe that you are basically a lovable, valuable person, you will be unable to trust others who claim they love you. If you believe that you must be perfect to be worthy of love and acceptance, then you are a candidate for a miserable life because you will never be perfect as long as you are in an earthly body.

You may have a perfect heart, in that your desire is to please God in all things, but your performance will not match your heart's desire until you get to heaven. You can improve all the time and keep pressing toward the mark of perfection, but *you will always need Jesus as long as you are here on this earth*. There will never come a time when you will not need His forgiveness and His cleansing blood.

Unless you accept your value and worth by faith through Christ, you will always be insecure and unable to trust those who want to love you. People who have no capacity to trust suspect the motives of others. I know this is true because I had a real problem in this area. Even when other people told me they loved me, I was always waiting for them to hurt me, disappoint me, fail me or abuse me. I figured that they must be after something; otherwise, they wouldn't be nice to me. I just could not believe that anyone would want me just for myself. There had to be some other reason!

I felt so bad about myself, was so full of shame, condemnation, self-hatred and self-rejection, that whenever anyone tried to show me love and acceptance, I thought to myself, "Well, if this person likes me now, they won't when they get to know the real me." Therefore I would not *receive* love from other people or from God. I deflected it by my behavior which became more and more obnoxious as I set out to prove to everyone that I was as unlovable as I believed myself to be.

Whatever you believe about yourself on the inside is what you will manifest on the outside. If you feel unlovely and unlovable, that is how you will behave. In my case, I believed that I was not loveable, so that is how I acted. I was very difficult to get along with. I believed that other people would eventually reject me, and so they usually did. Because my attitude was manifested in my actions, I could not sustain healthy, loving, lasting relationships.

The "Prove-You-Love-Me" Syndrome

Whenever anyone did try to love me, I heaped great pressure on that person to prove it to me — continually! I needed a "fresh fix" of "strokes" every day just to maintain a good feeling about myself. I had to constantly be complimented about everything I did; otherwise, I felt rejected. If I did not receive the reinforcement I craved, then I felt unloved.

I also had to have my way about everything. As long as other people agreed with me and gave in to my desires, I felt good about myself. However, if anyone disagreed with me or denied my requests, even to the slightest degree, it prompted an emotional reaction causing me to feel rejected and unloved.

I placed impossible demands on those who did love me. I frustrated them. I was never satisfied with what they were giving me. I could not allow them to be honest with me or to confront me. My entire focus was on me, and I expected everyone else's focus to be on me also. I was actually looking to people for my sense of self-worth, which is something that only God can give.

I have since learned that my sense of worth and value are in Christ, and not in things or other people. Until I learned that truth, however, I was very unhappy and totally incapable of maintaining healthy relationships.

Receiving the love of God is a key factor in emotional healing, as I mentioned in an earlier chapter. Once a person genuinely comes to believe that God, Who is perfect, loves him in his imperfection, then he can begin to believe that other people might love him also. Trust begins to develop, and he is able to accept the love that is being offered to him.

Since I have believed and received God's love for me, my most basic needs for love and a sense of self-worth have been met. I no longer require other people to keep me "fixed" all the time, that is, feeling secure about myself. Like everyone else, I do have needs that I want people to meet; we all need encouragement, exhortation and edification. But now there is no need to look to other people for affirmation of my value.

Now if my husband fails to compliment me on something I have done, I may be disappointed — but not devastated — because I know that I have value apart from what I do. Everyone likes to be recognized and complimented on what they do, but it is wonderful to be able to keep from falling apart if I don't receive that recognition and those compliments!

Once I learned that my value and worth are not in what I do, but in who I am in Christ, I no longer feel that I have to perform for people. I have decided that either they will love me for who I am, or they won't. Either way, I am secure knowing that God still loves me.

It is important to be loved for who we are and not for what we do. When we know that we have value in our identity rather than in our performance or behavior, we are able to get our minds off what others are thinking about us all the time. We can focus on them and their needs, instead of expecting their focus to be continually on us and our needs. This is the basis of healthy, loving and lasting relationships.

11
Confidence To Be an Individual

What is confidence? It has been defined as the quality of assurance that leads one to undertake something; the belief that one is able and acceptable; the certainty that causes one to be bold, open and plain.

If you think about this threefold definition, you will see why the devil attacks anyone who shows any degree of confidence.

People who have been abused, rejected or abandoned usually lack confidence. As we have already mentioned in previous chapters, such individuals are shame-based and guilt-ridden and have a very poor self-image.

The devil begins his assault on personal confidence whenever and wherever he can find an opening, especially during the vulnerable years of childhood — even while children are still in the womb. His ultimate goal is total destruction of the person. The reason is simple: An individual without confidence will never step out to do anything edifying to the kingdom of God or detrimental to Satan's kingdom, and therefore will never fulfill the plan of God for his life.

Expected Failure + Fear of Failure = Failure

Satan does not want you to fulfill God's plan for your life because you are part of his ultimate defeat. If he can make you think and believe that you are incapable, then you won't even try to accomplish anything worthwhile. Even if you do make an effort, your fear of failure will seal your defeat, which, because of your lack of confidence, you probably expected from the beginning. This is what is often referred to as the "Failure Syndrome."

No matter how many wonderful plans God has in mind for you, there is one thing you must know: *God's ability to bring His will to pass in your life is determined by your faith in Him and in His Word.* If you truly want to be happy and successful, then you must begin to believe that God has a plan for your life and that He will cause good things to happen to you as you put your trust in Him.

The devil wants you and me to feel so bad about ourselves that we have no confidence in ourselves. But here is the good news: *We don't need confidence in ourselves — we need confidence in Jesus!*

I have confidence in myself only because I know that Christ is in me, ever present and ready to help me with everything that I attempt to do for Him. A believer without confidence is like a large jumbo jet parked on the runway with no fuel; it looks good on the outside but has no power on the inside. With Jesus inside us, we have the power to do what we could never do on our own.

Jesus died for our weaknesses and inabilities, and He is willing to impart to us His strength and ability as we place our confidence (our faith) in Him. In John 15:5 He teaches us this important principle: . . . **apart from Me [cut off from vital union with Me] you can do nothing.**

Once you learn this truth, your response to the devil's lie, "You can't do anything right," can be, "Perhaps, but Jesus in me can; and He will, because I am relying on Him, and not on myself. He will cause me to succeed in everything that I put my hand to." (Josh. 1:7.)

Or should the enemy say to you, "You're not able to do this, so don't even try, because you will only fail again, just as you have in the past," your response can be, "It's true that without Jesus, I am not able to do one single thing; but with Him and in Him I can do all that I need to do." (Phil. 4:13.)

Whenever the devil reminds you of your past, remind him of his future. If you read the Bible all the way through to the end, you will see that the devil's future is very bleak. Actually, he is already a defeated foe. Jesus triumphed over him on the cross and made a public display of his disgrace in the spirit realm. (Col. 2:15.)

Satan is operating on borrowed time, and he knows it better than anybody. The only power he has over us is what we give him by believing his lies.

Always remember: *The devil is a liar!* (John 8:44.)

The Lie About Self-Confidence

Everyone talks about self-confidence. All kinds of seminars are available on confidence, both in the secular world and the church world. Confidence is generally referred to as "self-confidence" because we all know that we need to feel good about ourselves if we are ever to accomplish anything in life. We have been taught that all people have a basic need to believe in themselves. However, that is a misconception.

Actually, we don't need to believe in ourselves — we need to believe in Jesus in us. We don't dare feel good about ourselves apart from Him. When the Apostle Paul instructs us to put no confidence in the flesh (Phil. 3:3), he means just what he says — do not put confidence in yourself, or in anything you can do apart from Jesus.

We do not need self-confidence, we need God-confidence!

Many people spend their whole lives climbing the ladder of success only to find that when they get to the top, their ladder was leaning against the wrong building. Others struggle, trying to behave well enough to develop a measure of confidence in themselves, only to endure repeated failures. Both of these activities produce the same results: emptiness and misery.

I have found that most people fall into one of two categories: (1) They never accomplish anything, no matter how hard they try, and end up hating themselves because of their lack of achievement, or (2) they have enough natural talent to accomplish great things, but take all the credit for their achievements, which fills them with pride. Either way, they are a failure — in the eyes of God. The only truly successful person in God's eyes is the individual who knows he is nothing in himself, but everything in Christ. Our pride and boasting are to be in Jesus alone, and He is to have all the glory (credit due) for whatever accomplishments we may achieve.

In actuality, every person does have confidence (faith). The Bible confirms this fact in Romans 12:3. We are all born with a certain amount of faith; the important thing is where we put it. Some put their faith in themselves, some in other people, some in things — and then there are those who actually put their faith in God.

Don't be concerned about yourself, your weaknesses or your strengths. Get your eyes off of yourself and onto the Lord. If you are weak, He can strengthen you. If you have any strength, it is because He gave it to you. So either way, your eyes should be on Him and not on yourself.

Without true confidence (in Jesus), you will create many complicated problems for yourself. Here is a partial list:

1. You will never reach your full potential in Christ (as we have discussed in detail).

2. Your life will be ruled by fear and filled with torment.

3. You will never know true joy, fulfillment or satisfaction.

4. The Holy Spirit is grieved because He is sent to bring God's plan to pass in your life, and He never is able to do it without your cooperation.

5. You will open for yourself many doors of endless torment: self-hatred, condemnation, fear of rejection, fear of failure, fear of man, perfectionism, people-pleasing (which eliminates the possibility of being a God-pleaser), control and manipulation by others, etc.

6. You will lose sight of your right to be an individual — the right to be yourself.

This last danger, number six, is the one I would like to examine now. We have looked at the others to some degree in the first part of the book, but this last one is of major importance and deserves more consideration.

Confidence To Be an Individual

In 1 Corinthians 3:16,17 Paul teaches us that all of us make up one body, yet each of us is an individual member of that body. In Romans 12:4-6 he says almost the same thing, but in a little different way. This is a truth that is very important for us to grasp because we make ourselves miserable and stifle the power of God in us when we try to be something or someone we were not designed to be.

We have often heard it said that we all came out of different molds, meaning that no two of us are exactly alike. What's wrong with that? Nothing! God had a purpose in creating each of us differently. If He had wanted us to be alike, He could easily have made us that way. Instead, our uniqueness was so important to Him that He even went to the extreme of giving each of us a different set of fingerprints!

Being different is not bad, it is God's plan!

We are all part of one plan, God's plan. Yet each of us has a different function, because each of us is an individual.

I define "individual" as separate, distinguished by specific attributes or identifying traits, to be distinct or unique.

For years I thought I was *weird* — now I know that I am *unique!* There is a big difference. If I were "weird," it would indicate that something about me got messed up and did not turn out the way it should have; while my being "unique" indicates that there are no others like me, and therefore I have special value. You should believe that you are unique, special and valuable.

Don't Try To Be Someone Else

One of my identifying traits is my voice. Most women have soft, sweet voices, but mine is deep. Quite often when someone who does not know me calls our home, he will think the man of the house has answered the phone. I wasn't always comfortable with this very unique trait; in fact, I was insecure about it. I thought my voice was just plain weird! When God called me to teach His Word, and I began to realize that I would one day be speaking over public address systems (loud speakers) and even have a radio ministry, I was terrified! I thought that surely I would be rejected because I sounded so different from the way I *thought* a woman should sound. I was comparing myself with what I perceived as normal.

Have you ever compared yourself with someone else? How did it make you feel?

We are not to compare ourselves with others, but let Jesus be our example and learn to reflect the presence and personality of the God Who indwells us.

Diamonds have many facets. God is like a flawless diamond, and each of us represents a different facet of Him. He has placed a part of Himself in each of us, and we corporately make up His Body. What if our bodies were totally made up of mouths or ears, arms or legs? We would have no trouble speaking or hearing, carrying or walking, but what about the other functions? What a mess we would be if it had been God's intention to make us all exactly alike.

Why is it that we struggle so much trying to be like someone else, instead of simply enjoying who we are? Because we believe the lies of the devil. We believe him, that is, until we hear the truth of God's Word, and the truth that we believe sets us free.

God's grace will never be available to you to become another person. He created you to be you — the best *"you"* you can be! Forget about trying to be someone else. That is always a mistake, because usually the person you choose to be like, the person who "has it all together," is not the way you think. Let me give you some examples:

Example One

At one point in my life I decided that my pastor's wife was the "ideal woman." She was (and still is) a sweet lady: petite, cute, blonde, soft-spoken, gentle, mild and endowed with the gift of mercy. I, on the other hand, with my deep voice and straightforward, blunt personality, did not seem very sweet, gentle, mild or merciful. I tried to be that way, without much success. I actually attempted to lower the volume level of my voice and change the sound of it to seem more "feminine," but I only ended up sounding phony.

This lady and I could not seem to get along. Though we wanted and tried to be friends, it just did not seem to work out. Finally, a confrontation between us revealed that I was not really enjoying her because her presence put me under pressure to be like her. The really interesting thing that we both discovered was that Satan had sold her the same pack of lies I had bought; she was struggling to be more like me! She was trying to be less fragile and more forceful, to deal with people and things more directly and with greater boldness. It is no wonder that we could not have a successful relationship — we were each being pressured by the other!

Remember this: *God said that we "shall not covet" (*Ex. 20:17 KJV*)) — and that includes someone else's personality.*

Example Two

My next-door neighbor was a sweet girl who was gifted in many different ways. She sewed, had a garden and canned vegetables, played guitar and sang, did various kinds of arts and crafts, wallpapered, painted, wrote songs — in short, all the things I could not do. Since I thought I was "weird" anyway, I did not appreciate the talents I did have. I only thought about what abilities I lacked and all the things I could not do.

Since I was called by God to teach and preach His Word, my desires were different from those of many of the women I knew. While they were attending interior decorating parties, I was home praying. I was very serious about everything. It seemed to me that there was something very heavy going on inside me. While other women were relaxing and having a good time, I was constantly comparing myself to them, always feeling that something had to be wrong with me. This kind of feeling occurs when people are shame-based and insecure about who they are in Christ.

I did need to learn to "lighten up" a bit and have some fun, but God was doing something in me that needed to be done. He was causing me to see the mess that some people's lives were in, and calling me to help them out of that mess through His Word. I needed to be affected by the weight and seriousness of other people's problems.

I was in a waiting period during which God was not using me; it was a time of preparation, stretching and growing which lasted about one full year. During that year I decided it was time for me to become what I called a "regular woman." I bought a sewing machine and took some sewing lessons. I hated it, but forced myself to continue. Sewing was not something at which I excelled either. When a person has not been gifted in an area, he is just plain no good at it.

Sewing was such a struggle for me! I kept making mistakes that caused me to feel even worse about myself. I finally managed to get through enough sewing lessons to make a few garments for my family, which they dutifully wore.

I also decided that I should grow and can tomatoes. They were just beginning to look good, almost ready to be harvested, when a swarm of bugs attacked them overnight and left huge black holes in all of them! But I was determined to can tomatoes because I had already purchased all the canning equipment. So I went to the farmers' market and bought a bushel of tomatoes! I worked and sweated, sweated and worked, until I finally got those tomatoes canned! Once again, I hated and despised every second of it, but thought I was proving that I was "regular."

Through these very painful experiences, I learned that I was miserable because God would not help me be something that He had not created me to be. I am not to be someone else — I am to be me, just as you are to be you.

Be Yourself!

You have a right to be yourself! Do not let the devil steal that right from you!

If someone you know is a good Christian example in manifesting the character of the Lord or the fruits of the Holy Spirit, you may want to follow his example. The Apostle Paul instructed the Corinthians to follow him even as he followed the Lord. (1 Cor. 11:1 KJV.) Following a person's example is entirely different from trying to be like that individual in personality or gifts.

I strongly encourage you to think this over: Are you accepting the fact that you were not created like everyone else, that you are a unique individual? Are you enjoying your uniqueness, or are you at war with yourself as I was?

So many people are waging a private war inside themselves, comparing themselves to almost everyone they come near, which causes them to judge themselves or the other person. They conclude either that they should be like other people, or that others should be like them.

Lies!

None of us should be like anyone else. Each of us should be the facet of the Lord that He intends for us to be — uniquely individual — so that corporately we may accomplish God's plan and bring glory to Him.

12
Forgiveness

Receiving forgiveness for past mistakes and sins, and forgiving others for their mistakes and sins, are two of the most important factors in emotional healing.

Forgiveness is a gift given to those who do not deserve it.

God wants to begin the process by giving us the gift of forgiveness first. When we confess our sins to Him, He forgives us of our sins, puts them away from Him as far as the East is from the West, and remembers them no more. (1 John 1:9; Ps. 103:12; Heb. 10:17.) But for us to benefit from that forgiveness, we must receive it by faith.

Many years ago when I was first developing my relationship with the Lord, each night I would beg His forgiveness for my past sins. One evening as I knelt beside my bed, I heard the Lord say to me, "Joyce, I forgave you the first time you asked, but you have not *received* My gift because you have not forgiven yourself."

Have you received God's gift of forgiveness? If you have not, and you are ready to do so, ask the Lord to forgive you for all your sins right now. Say this aloud: "I receive Your forgiveness, Lord, for the sin of _____ (name the sin)." It may be difficult to verbalize some of your mistakes and sins from the past, but speaking them forth helps bring the release you need.

One time as I was praying, I asked God to forgive me because (as I put it), "I missed it."

"Missed what?" He asked.

"Well, You know, Lord," I answered, "You know what I did."

He did, indeed, know. But for my sake it was made clear to me that I needed to verbalize my sin. The Lord showed me that the tongue is like a dipper reaching down into a well within us and bringing up and out whatever is down there.

Once you clearly ask for the gift of forgiveness, receive it as your own and repeat out loud: "Lord, I receive forgiveness for _____ (name the sin), *in Christ Jesus*. I forgive myself, by accepting as my own, Your gift of forgiveness. I believe that You remove the sin from me completely, putting it at a distance where it can never be found again . . . as far as the East is from the West. And I believe, Lord, that You remember it no more."

You will find that speaking aloud is often helpful to you because by doing so you are declaring your stand upon God's Word. The devil cannot read your mind, but he does understand your words. Declare before all the principalities, powers and rulers of darkness (Eph. 6:12 KJV) that Christ has set you free and that you intend to walk in that freedom.

When you speak, sound as though you mean it!

If the devil tries to bring that sin to your mind again in the form of guilt and condemnation, repeat your declaration, telling him: "I was forgiven for that sin! It has been taken care of; therefore, I take no care for it." Satan is a legalist, so if you want to, you can even quote the date on which you asked for and received God's promised forgiveness.

Don't just sit and listen to the devil's lies and accusations; learn to talk back to him!

Confess to One Another Your Faults

Is anyone among you afflicted (ill-treated, suffering evil)? He should pray. Is anyone glad at heart? He should sing praise [to God].

Is anyone among you sick? He should call in the church elders (the spiritual guides). And they should pray over him, anointing him with oil in the Lord's name.

And the prayer [that is] of faith will save him who is sick, and the Lord will restore him; and if he has committed sins, he will be forgiven.

Confess to one another therefore your faults (your slips, your false steps, your offenses, your sins) and pray [also] for one another, that you may be healed and restored [to a spiritual tone of mind and heart]. The earnest (heartfelt, continued) prayer of a righteous man makes tremendous power available [dynamic in its working].

James 5:13-16

This passage can be referring, I believe, to any kind of sickness — physical, mental, spiritual or emotional. In verse 16, the way to be healed and restored is made very clear: "Confess to one another therefore your faults."

Does this mean that every time we sin, we need to confess it to another person? *No!* It does not mean that. We know that Jesus is our High Priest. We do not have to go to people to receive forgiveness from God. That was the case under the Old Covenant but not under the New Covenant.

What is the practical application of James 5:16? I believe we not only need to know the Word of God, but how to apply it practically to our daily lives. A person can be bleeding and know that he has a bandage, but if he does not know how to apply the bandage, he can bleed to death. Many people have the Word of God, yet they are "bleeding to death" (living in torment), because they do not know how to apply the Word in everyday situations.

I believe that James 5:16 should be applied in this manner. First, be sure you know that man cannot forgive sin — that is God's job. Yet, man can pronounce and declare God's forgiveness to you. Man can agree with you concerning your forgiveness. He can even pray for you to be forgiven. (1 John 5:16.) An example would be Jesus on the cross praying for those who had persecuted Him to be forgiven.

When do you need to apply this passage? I believe a time to consider placing James 5:16 into action is when you are being tormented by your past sins. Being poisoned inwardly keeps you from getting well — physically, mentally, spiritually or emotionally.

Once exposed to the light, things hidden in darkness lose their power. People hide things because of fear. Satan pounds at the mind with thoughts such as: "What will people say if they learn that I was abused?" "Everyone will think I'm horrible!" "I'll be rejected," etc. In my meetings, numerous people have come to me for prayer, confiding in me, "I have never told this to anyone, but I feel I need to get it out of my system; I was abused." Often they weep uncontrollably. With this weeping, however, often there comes a release that is desperately needed. Hurting people feel safe with me because they know that I was abused also.

Now, *please* understand that I am not saying that everyone needs to admit to being abused and to ask for prayer for healing. If you are suffering from the effects of abuse, be led by the Holy Spirit, not only in deciding whether you need to confess to someone, but also in deciding to whom you should make your confession. The person must be carefully chosen. I suggest a mature Christian you know you can trust. If you are married and your spouse fits this criteria, consider him or her first.

You should know that often when a spouse finds out about the situation, he or she will respond with anger toward the abuser. Therefore before you make your confession you should be sure that your spouse is Spirit-controlled and willing to follow God's leading and not personal feelings.

Your spouse may ask you some questions that you can easily misunderstand if you are not fully prepared for them. For example, when I told my husband about my father sexually abusing me all those years, he asked me, "Did you ever try to get him to stop?" and "Why didn't you tell anyone?" Keep in mind that your spouse may not fully understand your situation and feelings and may just need some answers. In my case, as soon as I explained to my husband that I was controlled by fear, he understood.

The practice of confessing our faults to one another and receiving prayer is a powerful tool to help break bondages. I had been having trouble with jealousy in a certain area for some time and I certainly did not want anyone to know about it, so I refused to ask for prayer. Instead, I chose to fight it out alone, and as a result made no progress at all. As God gave me revelation on James 5:16, "Confess to one another therefore your faults," I came to realize that there were a few areas in my life that were maintaining power over me, simply because I was hiding them and was too proud to bring them out in the open.

Fear can cause us to hide things, but pride can do that too. I humbled myself and confessed my problem to my husband, and he prayed for me. After that, I began to experience freedom in that area.

A Final Word

One last word of caution. Sometimes people relieve themselves of a problem and, in the process, give the problem to someone else. After hearing me teach on the importance of truth, and how hiding things can cause problems, a woman who attended our meetings came to me to confess that she had always disliked me intensely, and had even been gossiping about me. Then she asked me to forgive her, which, of course, I was willing to do. She left excited that she was rid of her problem, but I was left fighting off bad thoughts about her. I wondered what she had been saying about me, to whom she had been talking, if they had believed her and how long this had been going on.

Balance, wisdom and love are key words in the Bible. Operating in these qualities will accelerate your progress. A person who is filled with wisdom and love will think a matter through, seek and receive direction from the Lord, and handle the situation in a balanced way.

13

Forgiving Your Abuser

For many people, forgiving the one who abused them is the most difficult part of emotional healing. It can even be the stumbling block that prevents healing. Those who have been badly wounded by others know that it is much easier to say the word "forgive" than it is to do it.

I have spent a great deal of time studying and praying about this problem, asking the Lord for practical answers to it. I pray that what I have to say to you on this subject will be a fresh approach to a major issue that must be dealt with.

First, let me say that it is not possible to have good emotional health while harboring bitterness, resentment and unforgiveness.

Unforgiveness is poison!

It poisons anyone who holds it, causing him to become bitter.

And it is impossible to be bitter and get better at the same time!

If you are a victim of abuse, you have a choice to make. You can let each hurt or problem make you bitter or better. The decision is yours.

How can a hurt or problem make you a better person? God does not bring hurts and wounds upon you, but once they are inflicted upon you, He is able to cause them to benefit you if you will trust Him to do so.

God can make miracles out of mistakes!

Satan intends to destroy you, but God can take whatever the devil sends against you and turn it to your good. You must believe that or you will despair. As the psalmist wrote long ago, **[What, what would have become of me] had I not believed that I would see the Lord's goodness in the land of the living!** (Ps. 27:13).

Recently I received a letter from a woman who wrote, "I know God didn't cause your abuse, but if you had not been abused, you could not have helped me." She continued: "Please don't feel too badly about it, because God is using your pain to set others free."

Many years ago I had a choice. I could choose to remain bitter, full of hatred and self-pity, resenting the people who had hurt me as well as all those who were able to enjoy nice, normal lives, those who had never been hurt as I was. Or, I could choose to follow God's path, allowing Him to make me a better person because of what I had been through. I thank Him that He gave me grace to choose His way rather than Satan's way.

God's way is forgiveness.

I remember when I first started trying to walk with God. One evening I realized that I could not be full of love and hate at the same time. So I asked the Lord to remove the hate from me that had been there for so long. It seemed as though He reached down inside me and just scooped it out. After that experience, I never hated my father again. I still resented him, disliked him and was unable to bring myself to forgive him for what he had done to me. I wanted to be free from all the sour feelings and bad attitudes inside me, but the "how to" was a big question for me.

As I continued to study and meditate on the Word of God and to fellowship with the Holy Spirit, the Lord taught me many things. I would like to share with you what I have learned in the years of my progression toward complete healing.

Steps to Emotional Healing

First, you must choose God's way. He will not force it on you. If you want to lead a victorious life and enjoy full emotional health, you must believe that God's way is best. Even if you do not understand it, *choose* to follow it. It works.

Next, learn about God's grace. Grace is the power of the Holy Spirit that comes to us to help us accomplish God's will. James says, **But He gives us more and more grace (power of the Holy Spirit, to meet this evil tendency and all others fully). This is why He says, God sets Himself against the proud and haughty, but gives grace [continually] to the lowly (those who are humble enough to receive it)** (James 4:6).

(I have a six-tape album of teaching entitled "Grace, Grace and More Grace.")

You may choose to forgive and yet still have to struggle with frustration because you are attempting to forgive on your own strength, when you need the strength of the Lord. The prophet Zechariah tells us that it is . . . **Not by might, nor by power, but by My Spirit . . . says the Lord of hosts** (Zech. 4:6). After choosing to forgive, and realizing that you cannot forgive without God's help, pray and release the person who hurt you. Repeat this prayer aloud: "I forgive _____ (name) for_____ (whatever was done to you). I choose to walk in Your ways, Lord. I love You, and I turn this situation over to You. I cast my care upon You, and I believe You for my total restoration. Help me, Lord; heal me of all the wounds inflicted upon me."

There are many Scriptures that tell us that God vindicates. (Is. 54:17.) God is the One Who recompenses us. He is our reward. (Is. 35:4.) He is a God of justice, which only He can bring. He alone can repay you for the hurt done to you, and He alone is qualified to deal with your human enemies.

Beloved, never avenge yourselves, but leave the way open for [God's] wrath; for it is written, Vengeance is Mine, I will repay (requite), says the Lord.

Romans 12:19

For we know Him Who said, Vengeance is Mine [retribution and the meting out of full justice rest with Me]; I will repay [I will exact the compensation], says the Lord. And again, The Lord will judge and determine and solve and settle the cause and the cases of His people.

It is a fearful (formidable and terrible) thing to incur the divine penalties and be cast into the hands of the living God!

Hebrews 10:30,31

One of the main truths the Lord spoke to me while I was dealing with the forgiveness issue was this: "*Hurting people hurt people!*"

The majority of abusers were themselves abused in one way or another. Often those who were raised in dysfunctional homes create a dysfunctional atmosphere in their own homes.

When I looked at my own life, I saw the pattern. I had grown up in a dysfunctional home, so I was creating a dysfunctional atmosphere in my own home. I did not know any other way to behave. This realization was a tremendous help to me.

Hurting People Hurt People!

I really do not believe that my father understood what he was doing to me emotionally, nor do I believe that he realized he was causing a problem for me with which I would be dealing most of my life. He was doing what many people do who are not born again — living selfishly, satisfying their own perverted and demon-controlled desires, with no regard for the consequences of their actions. My father was simply determined that he was going to get what he wanted no matter what it did to me or anyone else.

We should remember what Jesus said as He hung on the cross suffering for things that were not His fault but were the fault of others, including the very ones responsible for His torment: . . .**Father, forgive them, for they know not what they do** . . . (Luke 23:34).

It is easy to judge, but the Bible tells us that mercy triumphs over judgment. I don't mean that abusers are not accountable for their sins — we all must be willing to take responsibility for our own wrongdoing. The Lord shared with me that mercy sees the "why" behind the "what." Mercy and compassion don't look just at the wrongdoing, they look beyond to the person doing the wrong — to the childhood, the temperament, the entire life of the individual. We must remember that God hates sin, but loves the sinner.

I had so many problems in my personality that it caused many people to judge and reject me. Jesus never rejected me, nor did He judge me. My sin was judged for what it was, but God knew my heart. Sin is sin, and my actions were wrong, no matter what caused them. But God knew that as a woman abused for fifteen years during her childhood, I was acting out major wounds — and He had mercy on me.

Isaiah prophesied of the coming Messiah: . . . **He shall not judge by the sight of His eyes, neither decide by the hearing of His ears** (Is. 11:3).

Often in my teaching, I show people the rock pictured on the next page. Hard, ugly and crusty on the outside, it is magnificently beautiful on the inside.

Crusty Exterior
of Rock

Beautiful Inside
of Rock

Looking only at the exterior, who would ever think that all that amazing beauty lay just below the surface? That is the way people are. God sees the inside. He sees the possibilities. He sees into the spirit. Everyone else sees the outer man. Unless we are trained by God to see beyond what can be perceived with the natural eye, we will always live with judgment in our hearts.

Remember: *Hurting people hurt people!*

14

Praying for and Blessing Your Enemies

But I tell you, Love your enemies and pray for those who persecute you.

Matthew 5:44

Invoke blessings upon and pray for the happiness of those who curse you, implore God's blessing (favor) upon those who abuse you [who revile, reproach, disparage, and high-handedly misuse you].

Luke 6:28

Bless those who persecute you [who are cruel in their attitude toward you]; bless and do not curse them.

Romans 12:14

As I began to minister to people, I noticed that quite often they would express a genuine desire to forgive their enemies but would admit that they were unable to do so. I went to God in prayer seeking answers for them, and He gave me this message: "My people want to forgive, but they are not obeying the Scriptures concerning forgiveness." The Lord led me to several passages about praying for and blessing our enemies.

Many people claim to forgive their enemies, but don't or won't pray for those who have hurt them. Praying for those who have wronged us can bring them to a place of repentance and a true realization of the harm they are causing others. Without such prayer, they may remain in deception. Pray for God to bless your enemies, those who abuse and ridicule and misuse you. You are not praying specifically for their works to be blessed, but rather for them to be blessed as individuals.

It is impossible for anyone to be truly blessed without knowing Jesus. As a victim of abuse, if you are willing to pray for your abusers, you will activate Romans 12:21: **Do not let yourself be overcome by evil, but overcome (master) evil with good.**

Ask God to show mercy, not judgment, to your abusers. Remember, if you sow mercy, you will reap mercy. (Gal. 6:7.) Blessing and not cursing your enemies is a very important part of the process of forgiveness. One definition of the word "bless" is to speak well of, and to curse means to speak evil of.

The Tongue and Forgiveness

When you have been mistreated, it is very tempting to talk to other people about what has been done to you. For the purpose of God-ordained counsel, this type of sharing is necessary. To receive healing, comforting prayer, it is also necessary to reveal what you have suffered at the hands of others. But to spread a bad report and ruin a reputation goes against the Word of God. The Bible teaches us not to gossip, slander or carry tales. The writer of Proverbs 17:9 says, **He who covers and forgives an offense seeks love, but he who repeats or harps on a matter separates even close friends.**

Quite often we exercise faith to receive healing from our hurts, and at the same time we fail to obey the royal law of love. In Galatians 5:6 the Apostle Paul tells us that faith works and is energized by love: **. . . for love covers a multitude of sins . . .** (1 Pet. 4:8).

We can have a talk with the Lord about what was done to us. We can even reveal it to those to whom it is needful or necessary for some reason. But if we want to forgive and recover from hurts and wounds, we must not talk loosely about the problem nor the person who caused it. The Bible warns us about vain (useless) conversation. (Matt. 12:36.) Unless revealing our problem has some godly purpose, we must discipline ourselves to bear it silently, trusting that God will reward us openly for honoring His Word.

I recall the case of a woman whose husband of more than thirty years became involved in an affair with her best friend. He disappeared with the woman, taking the family savings. This was a Christian family and, of course, the adultery and unfaithfulness were totally unexpected and shocking to everyone.

The devastated wife fell into the trap of talking about what her husband and friend had done to her, which was not an unnatural thing to do in the beginning. However, three years later, after she had received a divorce from her husband who had then married her friend, the woman was still not over the pain she had experienced. She married a wonderful man, who was very good to her, and she said that she wanted to forget the past and get on with her life, but she was unable to forgive and press on.

Listening to a set of my teaching tapes on the subject of the mouth and the power of words, she realized that she wasn't getting well because she was continually talking to anyone who would listen about what had happened to her. Going over and over the details, she was always recalling the painful memories.

God showed me that some people pray for healing and even say, "I forgive those who hurt me," so He begins a work, a healing process. But they won't allow Him to complete His work because they keep re-opening the wound.

When a physical wound begins to heal, a scab forms, but if it is continually picked off, the wound will never heal. It may even become infected and leave a scar. The same holds true with emotional wounds. Talking about the hurt and the person who caused it is equal to picking off a scab. It continually re-opens the wound and causes it to bleed again.

One of the most helpful things God has revealed to me is the fact that forgiveness requires a discipline of the tongue. The flesh always wants to "repeat or harp on a matter," but covering the offense will bring good results.

If you do need to talk about your problem for counseling, prayer or some other purpose, you can do it in a positive way.

Example: Which sounds more God-like?

"For fifteen years my father repeatedly abused me sexually. My mother knew about it and did nothing."

— Or —

"For fifteen years my father sexually abused me. God is healing me. I am praying for my father. I realize that he had hurts in his past and was controlled by demonic forces. My mother knew about what he was doing to me and should have helped me, but she was paralyzed by fear and insecurity. She probably didn't know how to face the situation, so she hid from it."

I am sure you agree that the second example sounds more loving. A few well-chosen words can change the entire flavor of a report. Remember, if you want to get better, you cannot be bitter. If there is any bitterness in you, it is highly likely that it will show up in your conversation. The tone of your voice and your choice of words can reveal a lot about you, if you are willing to be honest. In Matthew 12:34 Jesus says that . . . **out of the fullness (the overflow, the superabundance) of the heart the mouth speaks.**

If you want to get over a problem, stop talking about it. Your mind affects your mouth, and your mouth affects your mind. It is difficult to stop speaking of a situation until you stop thinking about it. It is also hard to stop thinking about it, if you continually talk about it.

Choose to do what you can do, and God will help you do what you cannot do.

It may take some time before you can discipline your tongue completely. Start by obeying the "promptings" of the Holy Spirit. If you receive conviction from Him to be quiet, obey and you will receive a bit more freedom each time you do so.

Also be aware that Satan will try to tempt you in this area. He knows the power of words. Words are containers for power! The mouth is a weapon either for Satan or against him. That's why you must choose your words carefully. Satan will even use well-meaning, loving friends to bring up your problem in conversation. Use wisdom and discretion. Don't be caught in a trap that will open up your wound and cause it to start bleeding again.

Trust God To Change Your Feelings

Feelings (emotions) are a major factor in the process of healing and the issue of forgiveness. You can make all of the correct decisions and for a long time not "feel" any different from the way you felt before you decided to be obedient to the Lord. This is where faith is needed to carry you through.

You have done your part and now you are waiting for God to do His. His part is to heal your emotions, to make you feel well and not wounded. Only God has the power to change your feelings toward the person who hurt you. Inner healing can be accomplished only by God because He, through the power of the Holy Spirit, lives in you (if you are born again), and He alone can heal the inner man.

Why does God make us wait for healing? Waiting is the difficult part. How well we wait reveals whether we have faith in God. According to Hebrews 6:12, the promises of God are inherited through faith and patience. In Galatians 5:5 the Apostle Paul states that we must . . . **by faith anticipate and wait for the blessing and good. . . .** We don't have to wait for results when we follow the flesh.

However, the natural human way of handling those who hurt us never produces good results.

God's way works, but it works on the principle of sowing seed and patiently waiting for the harvest. We sow seed by obediently following His plan, which is:

1. Choose to forgive.

2. Release those who hurt us by forgiving them.

3. Pray for our enemies.

4. Bless those who have hurt us.

5. Believe that God is healing our emotions.

6. Wait.

Waiting is where the battle is won in the spiritual realm. Waiting and keeping our eyes on God put pressure on the demonic forces that initiated the problem to begin with, and they have to give back the ground they have gained. As we keep our eyes on God, He forces the enemy off of our territory.

> **He who dwells in the secret place of the Most High shall remain stable and fixed under the shadow of the Almighty [Whose power no foe can withstand].**
>
> **I will say of the Lord, He is my Refuge and my Fortress, my God; on Him I lean and rely, and in Him I [confidently] trust!**
>
> **Psalm 91:1,2**

As you read the rest of Psalm 91, you will see that it is full of great promises about how the enemy cannot defeat you. Receiving the fulfillment of the promises in Psalm 91 depends on meeting the conditions of the first two verses. (See the footnote to Psalm 91 in *The Amplified Bible*.)

Here is an account of an experience I went through that will help clarify my point. A friend, someone I loved, trusted and had helped in many situations, hurt me very severely. Lies were spread about me that caused great trouble and anguish in my life. Judgment and gossip were involved, and the woman who was one of the major initiators of this mess should have known better.

This particular situation was probably the greatest emotional wounding I had ever experienced in my ministry, because it came from a co-laborer in Christ whom I trusted and with whom I worked. I knew I had to forgive her or else my unforgiveness would poison me and my ministry. I began the six-step process that I have been explaining to you. The first step, choosing to forgive, wasn't too difficult. Next, I prayed the prayer of forgiveness, which wasn't hard. The third step, praying for the woman herself, was a bit more difficult. But the fourth step, blessing her and refusing to talk about her, was probably hardest of all.

It actually appeared that she had gotten by with what she had done without any repercussions, while my feelings were in turmoil. I finally progressed to the point that I believed she was deceived by the devil, and that she had actually believed she was being obedient to God when she did what she did to me.

Although I was trying to apply step five, believing for my emotions to be healed, my feelings toward this woman did not change for six months. Step six, waiting on the Lord, was especially difficult for me because I had to be around this woman all the time. She never apologized for her actions or even indicated that she had done anything wrong. Sometimes I hurt so badly that I thought I could not stand it another day!

I would tell God, "I've done my part. I'm trusting You to change my feelings." I learned that, for the process to work, you have to stand your ground and not give up!

About six months went by. Sometimes when I saw this woman, I wanted to explode and tell her off! All I could do was keep asking the Lord to help me control myself. I went through various phases of emotions during those six months. At times I could be more understanding than at others.

One Sunday morning during a church service, I knew that God wanted me to go to this woman, hug her and tell her that I loved her. I can honestly say that my flesh was cringing. I thought, "Oh no, Lord, not that! Surely You won't require me to go to her when she should be coming to me! What if my going to her makes her think that I am admitting I was at fault?"

I wanted the woman to come and apologize to me, and yet I felt this gentle pressure to go to her. The Holy Spirit was trying to lead me into the blessings that God the Father had stored up for my life. So often the Lord tries to show us what will bless us, and we never receive the blessing because we are too stubborn to just do what He is showing us to do.

Finally I started toward the woman, hating every second of it in my flesh, but wanting to be obedient to the Lord. As I started toward her, she started toward me. Apparently God was speaking to her also.

When we met, I simply hugged her and said, "I love you." She did exactly the same thing, and that was the end of it. She still has never apologized to me, nor even mentioned what happened; however, for me obeying, God broke the yoke of bondage. As far as I was concerned, the whole incident was over, at least for the most part. Occasionally I felt a twinge of pain when I would see this woman, or when someone would mention her name, but I was never emotionally tormented by the situation from that day forward.

My advice to you, advice that has been gained from experience is:

Obey God and do things His way!

It may be hard sometimes, but it is harder to stay in bondage.

Always remember that statement. It is one of my favorite things the Lord has taught me:

Even though it hurts to get free, it hurts more to stay in bondage.

15

Back Pay for Past Hurts

Any time you are hurt by another person, there is always the feeling that he or she owes you. Likewise, when you hurt someone else, you may have a sense that you need to make it up to him, or pay him back in some way. Unjust treatment, abuse of any kind, leaves an "unpaid debt" in the spirit realm. Such "debts" are felt in the mind and the emotions. If they become too heavy and are allowed to stay around too long, you may even see bad results in your body because of all the things you feel others owe you and you owe them.

Jesus taught His disciples to pray, "Father, forgive us our debts, as we forgive our debtors." (Matt. 6:12 KJV.) He was speaking about asking God to forgive our sins, and He referred to them as "debts." A debt is something that is owed by one person to another. Jesus said that God will forgive us our debts — release them and let them go; act toward us as if we had never owed Him anything.

He also commanded us to behave the same way toward those who are in debt to us. Once again, let me say that this may sound difficult, but it is much more difficult to hate someone and spend your entire life trying to collect a debt that the person can never pay.

The Bible says that God will give us our *recompense*. (Is. 61:7,8.) I never paid much attention to that word until a few years ago while studying in the area of forgiveness and releasing debts. "Recompense" is a key word for anyone who has been hurt. When the Bible says that God will give us our recompense, it basically means that God Himself will pay us back what is owed us!

Here are some Scriptures to look at concerning God's giving us our recompense:

> **Instead of your [former] shame you shall have a twofold recompense; instead of dishonor and reproach [your people] shall rejoice in their portion. Therefore in their land they shall possess double [what they had forfeited]; everlasting joy shall be theirs.**

> **For I the Lord love justice; I hate robbery and wrong with violence or a burnt offering. And I will faithfully give them their recompense in truth, and I will make an everlasting covenant or league with them.**
> **Isaiah 61:7,8**

Several Scriptures say that God is a God of recompense and that vengeance is His. Isaiah 49:4 is the one the Holy Spirit used in my life:

> **Then I said, I have labored in vain, I have spent my strength for nothing and in empty futility; yet surely my right is with the Lord, and my recompense is with my God.**

I certainly labored in vain for many years. The word "vain" means useless. Have you labored in vain, have your efforts been useless? Are you worn out physically, mentally and emotionally from trying to pay back all those who hurt you or all those whom you have hurt? Vengeance is a way of trying to pay people back for some harm they have caused. The problem is that it is in vain — it doesn't remove the hurt or restore the damage. It actually causes more.

Many times those you are hating and trying to take vengeance on are out having a good time, not even knowing or caring how you feel. Dear sufferer, this is laboring in vain. As the Scripture says, I had spent my strength for nothing, all my effort was futile until I learned to look to God for my recompense.

"Recompense" is a word similar in meaning to workmen's compensation. If you get hurt on the job while working for God, He repays you. "Recompense" also means reward. According to the Bible, God Himself is our reward (Gen. 15:1), but He also rewards us by doing special things for us, giving us "joy unspeakable" (1 Pet. 1:8 KJV) and the peace "that passeth all understanding." (Phil. 4:7 KJV.) He has blessed my life to such a degree that it is often hard to actually believe that it is really me who feels so good and is so blessed.

For a long time I was filled with hatred and resentment. I was bitter, had a chip on my shoulder and felt sorry for myself. I took out my feelings on everybody, especially those who were trying to love me.

You must remember that what you are full of, you also have to feed on. When you are filled with anger, bitterness and resentment, not only do you poison other relationships, but you poison yourself as well. What is in you will come out! In conversation, in attitude, even in body language and voice tone.

If you are full of poisonous thoughts and attitudes, there is no way to keep them from affecting your entire life. Turn the business of debt collecting over to the Lord Himself. He is the only One Who can do the job properly. Align yourself with His ways, and He will collect your debts and repay you for all your past hurts. It really is glorious to watch Him do it.

I'm Willing, But How?

Write down all the debts you owe and all those owed to you. I am speaking of debts in the spiritual realm, not financial debts. Write across all of them, *Canceled!* Say aloud, "No person owes me anything, and I owe no person anything. I cancel all debts and give them to Jesus. He is now in charge of paying back what is owed."

If you have hurt someone, you can certainly tell that person that you are sorry, and ask for forgiveness. Please don't spend your life trying to pay back others for what you have done to them — that is useless. Only God can make it up to them. Here is a practical example.

While I was raising my children, I was still having lots of emotional ups and downs due to abuse in my past. Having been hurt and not yet knowing God's ways of doing things, I ended up hurting my own children. I did a lot of screaming and yelling. I had a bad temper — and no patience whatsoever. I was just plain hard to get along with, and difficult to satisfy.

I laid down many rules for my children. I gave them love and acceptance when they followed my rules, and I got mad when they didn't. I was not very merciful. I did not realize that I was treating my children the way I had been treated as a child, which is what most people do who have been abused.

As a result of years of living in a war zone, my older son developed some personality problems and some emotional insecurities. There always seemed to be a spirit of strife between us and, in general, we just never got along with each other. Of course, after receiving the baptism of the Holy Spirit, and studying the Word of God, I wanted to repair the damage I had done. I wanted to make up to my son for the way I had treated him. You might say that I wanted to pay him back for the hurt I had caused.

How do you go about doing that realistically? I apologized, but where do you go from there? For a while I fell into the trap of thinking that I should give him everything he wanted; after all, now I was in his debt. My son has a strong personality and, at that time, he was not walking with the Lord. He learned quickly how to make me feel guilty. He was manipulating and controlling me emotionally, as well as trying to use my new relationship with the Lord to his advantage.

One day as I was attempting to correct him about his behavior, he responded by saying, "Well, I would not be this way if you had treated me right." My reaction was "normal" for me at that time; I retreated to another room to feel bad about myself. However, this time God showed me something. He said, "Joyce, your son has the same opportunity to overcome his problems that you do. You hurt him because someone had hurt you. You are sorry, you have repented, there is nothing more that you can do. You cannot spend the rest of your life trying to undo what has already been done. I will help him if he will let Me."

I knew I was to tell my son what the Lord had told me. I did, and made a decision that I would stop trying to pay him back. He went through a few rough years, but he finally got more serious with God and started on his own road toward healing and maturity. He is now one of my good employees at Life In The Word, and also one of my good friends, as well as my son and co-laborer in Christ.

I really encourage you to examine this area in your life and allow God to recompense you. His reward is great. There is always a time of waiting where the things of God are concerned, but if you will keep doing what you know God is asking you to do, your breakthrough will come. You will make mistakes; when you do, just repent and go on.

When a baby begins to learn to walk, he never does so without falling down lots of times. He just gets back up and starts again for his destination. Come to Jesus like a little child. He is holding out His arms to you —head in His direction. Even if you fall down lots of times, get up and keep on going.

Before this chapter comes to an end, I would like to reiterate this point: Not only do we fall into the trap of trying to pay back people who have hurt us, but sometimes we take out our hurt on others who actually had nothing to do with causing it.

For years I tried to collect my emotional debts from my husband, just because he was a man and I was in relationship with him. This is a widespread problem. Some women hate all men because some man hurt them. A boy who is hurt by his mother may grow up and spend the rest of his adult life hating and abusing women. This is a type of debt-collecting. Please realize that such behavior does not solve the problem and will never provide an inner sense of satisfaction that the debt is finally taken care of. There is only one way to cancel the debt, and that is God's way.

16
Jealousy

Jealousy is wanting what someone else has. The jealous person doesn't mind if others keep what they have, as long as he gets the same thing.

What causes jealousy? I believe that one of its major causes is insecurity, a lack of knowledge of what it means to be "in Christ."

The devil lies to us and tells us that other people are "better" than we are. He successfully deceives us with negative thought patterns such as: "If I could just have what he has," or, "If I could just be like her," or "If only I could do what they can do." We think that if we were like others then we would be as "good" as they are. This kind of wrong thinking causes us to become filled with jealousy and envy.

Envy is different from jealousy in that someone who is envious doesn't want others to have what he has. In other words, being as good as someone else isn't enough. That doesn't satisfy him; he wants to be better than the other person.

One of the Ten Commandments is, "Thou shalt not covet." (Ex. 20:17 KJV.) The Old Testament Law stated that a person had to earn God's favor by perfection and by continually offering sacrifices to make up for his imperfection. This was impossible! If people worked and struggled hard enough, they might be able to keep the first nine commandments. But that tenth one — "Thou shall not covet" — they could not keep, because it had to do with the heart and desire of the individual.

To be righteous by the standard of the Law, a person was required to keep all of the Law perfectly. Keeping "most of it" was not sufficient. Therefore, all people were trapped by the commandment against coveting their neighbor's house or his servants or anything else he might have. This one commandment, itself, speaks loudly and clearly of just how desperately mankind needed a Savior. We human beings had to have help or we could never stand clean before God.

Under the New Covenant, every person's worth and value is based strictly on being "in Christ" by virtue of believing in Him totally as everything that individual needs. Christ is our RIGHTeousness. We are made right, not by having what someone else has, but by faith in Jesus. Understanding this truth brings a sense of security and completely eliminates the need to be jealous or envious.

Parts of the Same Body

One of the best examples God has ever given me to get a point across came to me one day while I was teaching on jealousy.

Use your imagination and think of this: I have one body but it is made up of many different parts. Each of the various parts of my physical body is different. Each looks different, serves a different function and has different capabilities. Some parts are more visible, while some are hidden and rarely ever seen. (In 1 Corinthians 12 the Apostle Paul uses this same example by comparing the Body of Christ to our physical body.)

My finger gets to wear a ring and my eye gets the pleasure of seeing the finger wear that ring. However, the eye never gets to wear a ring. Now if the eye were to get jealous and begin to complain, and to want a ring of its own, and *if* God were to decide to keep the jealous eye happy by granting its request, just think what a mess my body would be! If the eye were wearing a ring, the head would have to be tilted in such a way that the eye could no longer give guidance to the rest of the body because it would be unable to see.

Therefore, point one is that when we are trying to be something God never intended for us to be, it prevents us from fulfilling our God-given function in the Body of Christ. Also if the eye were trying to wear a ring, it would be unable to enjoy seeing the ring on the finger, which is the pleasure God intended the eye to have. Remember: The finger gets to wear the ring, but the eye gets to see the ring. The eye was created to enjoy seeing what the rest of the body has been given.

Point two is obvious: When a person is trying to be something he was not intended to be, it prevents him from the *enjoyment* that would be his if he would take his rightful place in the body and be satisfied with fulfilling the part God designed for him.

I personally believe this is one reason so many people who are going to heaven are not enjoying the trip.

If you would like to have some fun with me for a few minutes, take a ring from your finger and attempt to wear it on your eye. You will get the message fast.

As I said, God dropped this example into my heart while I was teaching. He expounded on it by using hands and feet as a further illustration. Think of this: When my feet get new shoes, my hands are so glad that if my feet are not able to get the new shoes on without some help, *my hands help my feet into their new shoes!*

This is the way the body is supposed to act — no part being jealous or envious of another part. Each part knows that it is uniquely created for a purpose by its Creator. Each part enjoys the function it has been assigned in the body, realizing that in God's eyes no one part is any better than another.

Having a different function does not make one part inferior to another. Each part is free to enjoy its place and role and to *help other parts when needed* without any hesitation. The hand does not say to the feet, "Well, if you think I am going to help you get your new shoes on, you have another think coming! Actually, I think I should have shoes also, I am tired of only wearing gloves and rings. I want to have shoes of my own so I will be like you."

No! This is not the way the hands respond when the feet get new shoes and need help putting them on. And this is *not* the way we should respond when someone we know needs some help. We should be ready to give others all the help we can in order to see them become all they were intended to be and to enjoy all the blessings God desires to pour out upon them.

Ask yourself: "Am I wearing my ring on my eye, or my shoes on my hands?" If you are, no wonder you're miserable and lacking in joy.

In the third chapter of John's Gospel, the disciples of John the Baptist came to him and reported that Jesus was beginning to baptize as John had been doing and that now more people were going to Jesus than were coming to John. This message was carried to John in a wrong spirit; it was intended to make him jealous. The disciples who brought the report were obviously insecure and being used by the devil in an attempt to stir up some wrong feelings in John toward Jesus.

> **John answered, A man can receive nothing [he can claim nothing, he can take unto himself nothing] except as it has been granted to him from heaven. [A man must be content to receive the gift which is given him from heaven; there is no other source.]**
> **John 3:27**

What John was saying to his disciples was that whatever Jesus was doing, it was because heaven had gifted Him in that way. John knew what God had called him to do, and he knew what Jesus was called to do. He also knew that a person cannot go beyond his call and gifting. John was saying to his followers, *"Be content."* He knew that God had called him to be a forerunner for Jesus, to prepare the way for Him, and that when it was time for Jesus to come to the forefront, he had to begin to become less visible to the people.

Here are John's words to his disciples in reply to their statement regarding the crowds who were flocking to Jesus:

> **He must increase, but I must decrease. [He must grow more prominent; I must grow less so.]**
>
> **John 3:30**

What a glorious freedom!

It is a wonderful feeling to be secure in Christ and not have to be in competition with anyone.

Freedom From Competition

> **Let us not become vainglorious and self-conceited, *competitive* and challenging and provoking and irritating to one another, envying and being jealous of one another.**
>
> **Galatians 5:26**

In Galatians 6:4 the Apostle Paul exhorts us to grow in the Lord until we come to the point that we can . . . **have the personal satisfaction and joy of doing something commendable [in itself alone] without [resorting to] boastful comparison with . . .** other people.

Thank God, once we know who we are "in Christ," we are set free from the stress of comparison and competition. We know that we have worth and value apart from our works and accomplishments. Therefore we can do our best to glorify God — not to try to be better than someone else.

Quite often people ask my husband or me what it is like for Dave to be married to a woman who does what I am doing. I am the voice on the radio, the face on the television; I am the one who stands on the platform in front of the people; I am the one who is most seen and talked about. In other words, I am the focal point of our ministry. Dave is the administrator, an important function but a background position. His work is behind the scenes not out front as mine is.

Our situation is unique in that it is usually the other way around. Generally in a team effort, it is the man who occupies the focal position while his wife works behind the scenes to help him. My husband happens to be secure enough that his sense of worth or value is not affected by what he does or does not do. In fact, he is so secure that (in obedience to the Lord) he has been able to help me be all that I can be in Christ. He is content to help me fulfill the call of God on my life, and, in the process, is fulfilling God's claim on his own life.

What is Dave's call, and what does he do? His position is certainly just as important as mine. It is just not as noticeable by the public. As administrator for the ministry, he oversees the finances, locates and contracts with radio and television stations interested in carrying our Life In The Word broadcast, carefully watches over all the stations which already carry our broadcast to make sure they are bearing good fruit, and handles all of our travel arrangements.

At our meetings, Dave loves working behind the table where our teaching tapes are displayed, talking with the people and ministering to them. I have asked him numerous times to share the platform with me, and his reply has always been the same: "That is not where I am supposed to be. I know my place, and I am going to stay in it." That is the statement of a mature, secure man.

People have a tendency to ask Dave, "Are you Joyce's husband?" He usually replies, "No, Joyce is my wife."

Dave fulfills many, many important functions in our ministry, but in summing up his role, he usually says, "I am called by God to be Joyce's covering, to get her where God wants her to be. I make sure she does not get hurt, and I see to it that she does not get in trouble." Sometimes there are things I want to do that Dave will not allow because he feels they are unwise or that the timing is wrong. I will not say that it is always easy to submit to his desires, if they are not mine, but I have learned that his gifts bring balance to our lives and our shared ministry.

Dave wrestled with our situation for a couple of years in the beginning. Actually, he did not want to be in ministry at all. However, God showed him that He had given me the gift of teaching His Word. Dave says, "God did not ask me to submit to my wife, but He did ask me to submit to the gift He put in her." He says that God showed him that the gift was His and that by submitting to that gift and allowing me to do what He had called me to do, Dave was submitting to the Lord Himself.

Dave not only allows me to do what God has called me to do, he helps me do it. I consider it a great honor to be married to Dave Meyer. As far as I am concerned, he is the greatest man I know. He is also the happiest, most contented person I know. When I say that he is always happy, I mean it literally. He enjoys life to the fullest. I believe, and so does Dave, that this joy is a result of his submitting to God and not trying to become something that the Lord has not called him to be.

He is not in competition with anyone. He is not trying to prove anything to anyone.

Securely Rooted and Grounded

. . . May you be rooted deep in love and founded securely on love.

Ephesians 3:17

When we are free from the need to compete with other people, we are free to help them succeed. When we really know who we are, we don't have to spend our lives trying to prove our worth and value to ourselves or to others.

Dave knows he is important to God, and so what the world thinks of his position as compared to mine does not concern him at all. I believe that Dave's decision and life can be a testimony to many. There is much to be done in the kingdom of God, and it will best be accomplished if all of us work together in whatever individual capacity God assigns us.

Let us all lay aside *jealousy, envy, competition* and *comparison.* Remember, these problems are rooted in insecurity. The good news is that we can be free from insecurity and therefore free from the problems it causes. Isaiah 54:17 says in part: . . .**This [peace, righteousness, security, triumph over opposition] is the heritage of the servants of the Lord.** . . . That means that part of our inheritance as sons and daughters of God is security! Start spending your inheritance now.

Enjoy the contentment, satisfaction, peace and joy that come from knowing that God loves you and views you as righteous and valuable through your faith in His Son Jesus Christ. Be firmly rooted in and securely grounded on His love for you.

17

Emotional Addictions

Earlier in the book I mentioned the term "addictive behaviors" to describe the types of behavior that can develop when a person has been abused and has a shame-based nature. In this section, I would like to deal specifically with what I call "emotional addictions" and how to break them.

In this context, an *addiction* can be defined as compulsory behavior, often in response to some stimulus, without conscious thought. People who have been hurt tend to *react* rather than to *act*. What I mean is that they tend to react out of their wounded emotions, rather than to act according to wisdom and the Word of God.

For many years, whenever I was faced with a situation or a personality that reminded me of the past, I responded emotionally, reacting out of fear instead of acting on faith. These types of incidents can be very confusing to the wounded victim because everything happens so quickly that he really doesn't even understand why he is behaving as he is.

For example, the person who abused me had a very strong, domineering personality. I was subjected to a lot of manipulation and control during my childhood. I decided and repeatedly promised myself that when I was old enough to leave home and get out on my own, nobody would ever control me again.

In subsequent years, I had a warped view of authority. I saw all authority figures as my enemy. I was so fearful of being controlled and manipulated that when any person in my life tried to get me to do anything I did not want to do, I would react with rage or withdrawal. Often the incidents were very minor. Even a suggestion from someone that was not in line with my wishes could cause me to act very strangely. I had no more understanding of my actions than anyone else. Logically, I knew I was behaving badly; I did not want to act that way, but I seemed powerless to change.

God began to teach me about emotional addictions, showing me that in the same way that people can become addicted to certain chemical substances in their physical bodies (i.e., drugs, alcohol, nicotine, caffeine, sugar), they can also develop mental and emotional addictions. Remember, an addiction is "compulsory behavior done without thinking it through." My violent reactions were basically my way of saying to others, *"You are not going to control me!"*

I was so fearful of being controlled that I overreacted to every situation, trying to protect myself when there was no real problem. The rage said, "I will not let you control me!" And the withdrawal said, "I refuse to get involved with you!" A person cannot get hurt if he refuses to get involved. Therefore, whenever anything painful occurred in any of my relationships, I either attacked it or refused to deal with it at all. Both of these types of behavior are out of balance and unscriptural; they only increase the problem of addiction by feeding it.

If a person is addicted to drugs, then the more drugs he takes, the more he is likely to need. The longer he allows his addiction to control him, the more it demands from him. Eventually it will consume him. The addiction must be broken. And that means denying the flesh the substance it is accustomed to, and going through the pain of withdrawal in order to get free. The same principle applies to mental or emotional addictions.

Addicted to Worry and Reasoning

One of my mental addictions was worry. I worried and worried and worried. Even when there was nothing to worry about, I found something. I developed a false sense of responsibility, always attempting to solve problems for which I had no solution. I reasoned, figured and lived in constant confusion.

As a result, my mind was continually filled with worry and reasoning. Although it made me physically and mentally exhausted and stole any hint of joy in my life, I could not seem to control it. Worry and reasoning were my automatic responses to any problem. Although my behavior was abnormal, it was normal for me because that was the way I *always* reacted to problems.

The Word of God says, "Trust in the Lord. " (Ps. 37:3.) However, trust is not an easy thing if you have been abused. The people you trusted to take care of you didn't do it; instead they used you. They hurt you terribly, so you made a promise to yourself that nobody would ever hurt you again. You don't wait to discover whether others will hurt you or not, you simply put up walls of protection around yourself to shield yourself from harm.

One of the ways you protect yourself is by trying to figure out everything. If you can accomplish this, you have everything under control, and there are no surprises to upset you.

When God began to work in my life, He showed me clearly that I was addicted to worry and reasoning, and that I had to give them up. If there was a problem in my life, and I wasn't trying to solve it, then I felt totally out of control inside. You must remember that I wanted to be in complete control of everything that was going on around me — that way I thought I would not get hurt.

I believed that I would take good care myself, but I did not believe that anyone else would take care of me.

Deny Yourself

. . . If anyone intends to come after Me, let him deny himself [forget, ignore, disown, and lose sight of himself and his own interests] and . . . cleave steadfastly to Me.

Mark 8:34

As the Lord continued to work with me in His patient ways, He taught me that I could trust Him, that I could believe He was working on my problem even when I wasn't. My part was to step out in faith and refuse to worry or reason. I had to *deny* my mind the addictive behavior it was accustomed to; as I did so, eventually I was set totally free from it. I did have some withdrawal symptoms — feeling afraid, out of control, and even "stupid." (The devil will try anything to keep a person in bondage — even making him feel ridiculous.)

In Mark 8:34 Jesus teaches us that in order to follow Him, we must deny ourselves and our way and choose His way. My way was to take care of myself. His way is to deposit ourselves with Him and learn by experience that He will never fail us or forsake us. (Heb. 13:5.) In order to learn this truth, I had to first give up "my way."

Like a Weaned Child

Surely I have calmed and quieted my soul; like a weaned child with his mother, like a weaned child is my soul within me [ceased from fretting].

Psalm 131:2

Evidently the psalmist was aware of the same things we are discussing in this chapter on breaking addictions. He even mentions his *soul* being weaned. The soul is often defined as the mind, will and emotions. We see from this Scripture that these areas may become addicted to certain types of behavior just as the body may become addicted to certain types of substances.

By denying my mind the privilege of worrying and reasoning, I was weaned from my mental addiction just as a baby is weaned from its bottle or pacifier. And even as the baby has fits of crying and trying all sorts of ways to get the bottle or pacifier back, I also had fits of anger, crying and self-pity. I even had occasional attacks of fear, but I continued to conform myself to God's way until I was totally delivered from following my way.

Jesus said that He came to release the captives (Luke 4:18), and that he whom the Son has set free is free indeed! (John 8:36 KJV.)

18
Intimacy and Trust

For a person who has been abused, intimacy is often very difficult. Intimacy requires trust, and once the trust factor has been destroyed, it must be restored before intimacy will be comfortable.

Since people always hurt people, we cannot depend on others never to hurt us. I cannot tell you, *"Just trust people; they won't hurt you."* They may not intend to hurt you, but we may as well face the reality that "people hurt people."

As I have already mentioned, my husband is a wonderful, kind, easy-going man; yet there are times when he hurts me, just as there are times when I hurt him. Even people who love each other very much sometimes hurt and disappoint each other.

It took many years before I was comfortable being intimate with my husband and could honestly say that I enjoyed our sex life. I was so fearful of being hurt and taken advantage of that I could not relax. My basic attitude was, "If we must do this, then let's just get it over with, so I can forget it and go on to something else." Of course, my husband could sense my attitude, even though I tried to hide my true feelings and pretend that I enjoyed our sexual relationship.

My attitude made Dave feel rejected. Had he not been a mature Christian who had some discernment from the Lord about what was going on in me, my attitude could have done severe damage to his concept of himself as a man, let alone as a husband. He once said to me, "If I were depending on you to tell me what kind of a man I am, I would be in serious trouble."

I am grateful that the Lord gave me a mature Christian man for my husband. I am grateful that I did not destroy him while I was being healed. So often, troubled people marry troubled people. After they have destroyed each other, their problems are transferred to their children, who in turn become the next generation of troubled, tormented people.

For many years I evaded the issue. Deep down inside I knew that I needed to deal with my attitude regarding sex and intimacy, but I continued to *put it off* month after month, year after year. Do you have a tendency to put off things that God is trying to get you to deal with? We do that because some issues are too painful even to think about, much less go through.

Finally, I made the decision to stop procrastinating and to face the truth. In this situation the truth was as follows: (1) I had a problem that I was punishing Dave for. (2) He had been very patient with me, but it was time for me to deal with my problem. (3) As long as I continued to behave as I did, the devil would continue to defeat me because I was allowing my past to affect my present and my future. (4) Putting off dealing with the problem would be nothing more than direct disobedience to the Holy Spirit.

Of course, I was very much afraid; I did not even know how to begin. I remember crying out to God, "But how can You expect me to trust Dave? What if he takes advantage of me? Or what if . . ." The devil never runs out of *"what ifs."* I specifically remember the Lord saying to me, "I am not asking you to trust Dave; I am asking you to trust Me." This put a totally different perspective on the situation. It was easier for me to trust God than people, so that's where I started.

I simply committed to do whatever the Lord showed me in my heart I was to do and to trust Him with my feelings about it. For example: I always wanted the lights out while Dave and I made love. I recall that in my heart I came to realize that I should leave them on, and so I did. That was difficult, but once I did it a few times, it got easier and easier. Now I am free to leave the lights on or turn them off; it doesn't matter anymore because I am not hiding from anything.

Another example: I never, never would approach Dave to show any interest in having sex with him. There were times when I desired him; my physical body had a need, but I *would not* approach him. I began to realize that when I felt that I wanted him, I needed to take some action to let him know. This was particularly difficult for me because I always felt that sex was wrong or dirty because that was the way it had been initially presented to me in my childhood.

My first sexual experiences were perverted, so my attitude toward sex was perverted. Mentally, I knew that sex was originally God's idea, but I could not seem to get past my feelings. Once again, taking "obedient action" broke the bondage, and now I am free in this area also.

Please understand that when the Holy Spirit is prompting you to do something, He is doing it to help you, to bless you and to set you free in some way.

The Holy Spirit is the Helper and only has your good in mind.

People may hurt you, but God won't. Some of the things He leads you through may hurt for a while, but God ultimately will work them for your good.

As I continued this process of choosing to do what the Lord was showing me, I enjoyed progressive freedom, and so will you. There were many instances too numerous to mention here, but I think you understand what I am talking about. You will have your own situations to face, and the

Holy Spirit will walk you through your healing process concerning intimacy and trust.

Refuse to live the rest of your life in a prison of suspicion and fear!

Trust the Lord

I know I have said this in other places in this book, but I feel prompted to say it again. The main thing that helped me in this area of trust, as well as in other areas, was simply to realize that God is not asking us to put our trust in man, but in Him.

We can learn to trust people in a balanced way. If we get out of balance, we will get hurt. Often God uses these situations to teach us the wisdom of keeping relationships in balance.

In dealing with this issue, I often look to Jeremiah 17:5-8. Verse five begins: **Thus says the Lord: Cursed [with great evil] is the strong man who trusts in and relies on frail man, making weak [human] flesh his arm, and whose mind and heart turn aside from the Lord.** Think about this verse. It says bluntly that we are going to find curses (trouble) if we give man the trust that rightfully belongs to the Lord.

In verse six we find these words: **For he shall be like a shrub or a person naked and destitute in the desert; and he shall not see any good come, but shall dwell in the parched places in the wilderness, in an uninhabited salt land.** I believe the point is being well made that many are having trouble and are very unhappy, simply because they are looking to people to meet their needs when they should be looking to God.

The "arm of the flesh" mentioned in verse five can be referring to trusting self as well as trusting others. When I look to myself to meet my needs, I fail; and when I look to others to meet my needs, they fail me. The Lord requires

146

that He be allowed to meet our needs. When we look to the Lord, He often uses people to meet our needs, but we are looking to and depending on Him — not the people through whom He works — and this is the balance He requires of us.

Verse seven presents the good news: **[Most] blessed is the man who believes in, trusts in, and relies on the Lord, and whose hope and confidence the Lord is.** We see from this Scripture that great blessings will be ours when we trust God and put our confidence in Him.

There were times in the past when I would feel discouraged and get angry at the people around me because they were not giving me the encouragement I needed. As a result, I would have a resentful attitude of self-pity that my family and others could not understand. It certainly did not result in having my needs met because I was looking to people when I should have been looking to God.

The Lord taught me that when I needed encouragement I should ask Him for it. As I learned to do that, I discovered that He would provide the needed encouragement through the source He chose. I learned that it was not necessary for me to put pressure on relationships in an effort to get from people what only God could give me.

Finally, verse eight says that the person who puts his hope and confidence in the Lord . . . **shall be like a tree planted by the waters that spreads out its roots by the river; and it shall not see and fear when heat comes; but his leaf shall be green. It shall not be anxious and full of care in the year of drought, nor shall it cease yielding fruit.** This verse assures us that as we place our trust in God instead of the frail "arm of the flesh," we will become *stable*. I emphasize this word because it is very important to our discussion. There can never be any real enjoyment in life without a sense of stability.

Let these verses encourage you to place your trust in God and not in man.

Don't look to others to meet your needs, look to God. Anything people may do to you, God can fix.

One final thought concerning intimacy. God has created all of us to thoroughly enjoy one another. In particular, the Bible says that a husband and wife should enjoy each other. (Prov. 5:18.) Part of enjoying your spouse and your marriage is enjoying intimacy. Take a step of faith and realize that fear of being hurt is hurting you more than facing that fear and finding freedom. Trust God with the people in your life. You may not be able to handle them, but He is able.

The Importance of Balance in Relationships

Ask yourself if you have any relationships that are out of balance. Is there anyone in your life that you are depending on too much? When you have problems, do you run to the Throne or the phone? Are you looking to people to keep you happy, or are you looking to the Lord?

I recall a time when I was attacked by fear that something might happen to my husband. I began thinking, "What would I do if Dave died?" It was a panic-filled type of thinking, which was unusual for me. I had never even considered what I would do if Dave should die before I did. Like most women who have good marriages, I depend on my husband a lot. Dave is good to me, and as I thought of all the things he does for me, I became more and more panic-stricken. Then the Lord spoke this to me in the depths of my heart: "Joyce, if Dave died, you would keep on doing exactly what you are doing. It is not Dave who is upholding you and causing you to do what you are doing, it is Me; so put your trust in Me, where it belongs. Trust Dave, but don't get out of balance."

One final example I would like to share with you concerns a certain friendship and working relationship in my life. Sexual intimacy is not the only kind of intimacy that needs to be restored to wounded people. Those who have been abused often experience difficulty in maintaining any type of relationship. Not only is the marriage relationship affected, but Satan seeks to use their hurts and disappointments with people to ruin all their close relationships.

Like many others in the world, not only was I abused in my early years at home, but even after I had gotten away from that situation, I continued to be easily hurt — by nearly everyone I encountered. When I finally became part of the Church, I thought that surely church people would not hurt me. I soon discovered, however, that the pain did not stop just because I was a church member. In fact, in some instances, it became more severe. The result for me was that I did not trust men because it was a man who had hurt me, which affected my marital intimacy. I had also been hurt severely by friends and relatives at various times, so I honestly was afraid to trust anyone.

As the years went by and Dave and I got involved in full-time ministry, a couple came to work for us who were definitely sent by the Lord. They were and are anointed by God to be "armor-bearers" for us. That means that they pray for us regularly; they work side by side with us, and are available to do whatever needs to be done, whenever it needs to be done. They are very good to us, and they make our lives a lot easier.

The scope of our ministry would be much different if we did not have this wonderful couple, or someone like them, to help us. Because of the years of hurt I had experienced, I did not open my heart too readily, but as time passed, I came to trust these people very much and to depend on them quite heavily.

One day I read a Scripture in which the psalmist said something about a good friend lifting up his heel against him. (Ps. 41:9.) I knew that verse applied to me and began to wonder who the Lord was warning me about. I knew He was trying to show me something, because I kept supernaturally coming across the same Scripture repeatedly. I was convinced that God was saying something. I began to wonder if He was showing me that it was this couple who was going to hurt me.

Finally, the Lord made Himself clear enough for me to understand that He was just warning me not to let our relationship get out of balance. He taught me that we could have a close relationship, enjoy years of faithful, loyal service and produce a lot of good fruit for His Kingdom, but that I was being specifically warned not to "put a trust in them that belong to Him." He let me know that He had brought that couple into my life, and He could certainly take them away, which He would do if I put my eyes on them as my source of help instead of keeping them on Him.

Even intimacy in a good friendship is scriptural, but it must not get out of balance. Think of David and Jonathan. The Bible says that their souls were knit together. (1 Sam. 18:1.) They helped each other and enjoyed covenant relationship. Good friendship is very important, but so is balance. Why do I keep referring to the importance of balance? The Apostle Peter says, **Be well balanced . . . for that enemy of yours, the devil, roams around like a lion roaring [in fierce hunger], seeking someone to seize upon and devour** (1 Pet. 5:8). Stay in balance, and it won't be you or your relationship that the devil devours.

19

Free at Last

The pathway to freedom is not necessarily easy. However, pressing forward toward freedom is definitely easier than staying in bondage.

So, since Christ suffered in the flesh *for us, for you,* arm yourselves with the same thought and purpose [patiently to suffer rather than fail to please God]. For whoever has suffered in the flesh [having the mind of Christ] is done with [intentional] sin [has stopped pleasing himself and the world, and pleases God].

So that he can no longer spend the rest of his natural life living by [his] human appetites and desires, but [he lives] for what God wills.

1 Peter 4:1,2

Careful study of this Scripture passage reveals that we need to arm ourselves with proper thoughts such as: "I would prefer to suffer with Christ in order to do right, than to remain in bondage to sin."

Having the correct "mind-set" is important to victory. When I began to realize that Jesus could and desired to set me free, I wanted to lay hold on that freedom but my attitude was, "I will not suffer anymore; I have suffered enough, and I will not submit to anything that even remotely resembles emotional pain." The Holy Spirit led me to Scripture passages like this one which helped me realize that I had a wrong mind-set and needed to prepare myself or arm myself with right thinking.

I began to think this way: "I do not want to suffer anymore, but I will, rather than stay in bondage. As long as

I am in bondage, I am suffering anyway, but it is a type of suffering that has no end. If I am willing to let Jesus lead me through whatever I must go through in order to be free, it may hurt for a while but at least it will be a suffering that leads to victory, to a new life liberated from emotional pain."

A good example is physical fitness. If my body were terribly out of shape due to bad eating habits and a lack of exercise, I would be suffering because I would be tired and feel bad all the time. As long as I did nothing about my condition, the suffering would just continue day after day. If I decided to get in shape, I would start to exercise, choose the right foods and avoid the wrong ones.

For a period of time, I would suffer from sore muscles. My body might throw a fit if I didn't give it certain "addictive foods" that it was used to. That is a type of suffering. I would need to redirect some of my time to allow for exercise, and that might produce a certain type of suffering because I would need to make wise choices and not emotional choices.

We can see by this example that in order to be free from the senseless suffering that is produced by being physically unfit, a person must suffer in another way, but it is a type of suffering that leads to victory and ultimately brings an end to suffering.

Right Suffering and Wrong Suffering

Moreover [let us also be full of joy now!] Let us exult and triumph in our . . . sufferings, knowing that pressure and affliction and hardship produce patient and unswerving endurance.

And endurance (fortitude) develops maturity of character (approved faith and tried integrity). And character [of this sort] produces [the habit of] joyful and confident hope of eternal salvation.

> **Such hope never disappoints or deludes or shames us, for God's love has been poured out in our hearts through the Holy Spirit Who has been given to us.**
> **Romans 5:3-5**

Because of a wrong mind-set, many people never experience joy in living. Meditating on these Scriptures reveals that we should choose by faith to be joyful while we are going through difficult transitions, knowing that because God loves us, even our "right suffering" will produce a good end — in this case, mature character. Maturity always includes stability. Without stability we never really experience peace and joy.

There is a "right suffering" and a "wrong suffering." The Apostle Peter encouraged the people of his day to be sure that they did not suffer for wrongdoing, but that if they did suffer, it was for doing the right thing. In 1 Peter 3:14 he notes, **But . . . in case you should suffer for the sake of righteousness, [you are] blessed . . . .**

In verse sixteen he exhorts us to live in such a way that we make sure our conscience is entirely clear, and in verse seventeen he says, **For [it is] better to suffer [unjustly] for doing right, if that should be God's will, than to suffer [justly] for doing wrong.**

This is an important area because many people never experience the joy of freedom because of a wrong mind-set concerning suffering. At some point in your Christian life, you may have heard that Jesus wants to set you free from all your suffering, and that is true — He does. However, there is a transition involved, and transition is never easy.

During childbirth, the part of the labor process known to be the most difficult is called "transition." For thirty-three years I lived a life of pain. When I finally discovered that Jesus wanted to free me from suffering, I entered transition. I was being changed, transformed into His original idea of me before I was marred by the world. I suffered for a few more years, but in a different way. It was not a hopeless suffering but a suffering that actually produced hope because I could see changes throughout the transition.

These were not always big changes, but the Lord always kept me from giving up. Just when I thought I could not stand the pain any longer, He would come through with a special blessing that would let me know that He was there all the time — watching over me.

The Refiner's Fire

But who can endure the day of His coming? And who can stand when He appears? For He is like a refiner's fire and like fullers' soap;

He will sit as a refiner and purifier of silver; and He will purify the priests, the sons of Levi, and refine them like gold and silver, that they may offer to the Lord offerings in righteousness.

Malachi 3:2,3

If you understand them, these verses have special meaning that brings great comfort. I would like to share with you a story that I once heard which sheds light on this passage.

In Europe a man went into a goldsmith's shop and found some items he wished to buy. The entire time he was inside the shop, he never saw the shopkeeper. In order to finalize his purchases, he began to look for the proprietor, and as he did, he noticed in the rear of the shop an open door that led outside. As he stood in the doorway, he saw the shopkeeper (actually the refiner) sitting over a fire upon which sat a huge pot. He would not take his eyes off the simmering pot, even though the interested customer tried to speak to him about buying some of his merchandise.

The customer asked if he could not leave what he was doing for a short while to come inside and take care of the transaction. However, the refiner said, "No." He stated that he could not leave the metal in the pot, not even for one minute, explaining it this way: "It is very important that this metal, which is gold, does not harden until all the impurities are out of it. I intend for it to be pure gold. If the fire gets too hot, it could ruin it, and if the fire gets too cool, the gold could harden with impurities still in it."

He explained that he could not leave it, nor take his eyes off it at all. He would need to sit over it until it was completely finished. The customer asked when that would be, and the refiner replied, "I will know it is finished when I can look in the metal and see my reflection very clearly."

To me, this is such a beautiful story because it lets me know that God is always guarding my life and watching over the trials that come my way to make sure they don't become too intense. But He also makes sure there is enough pressure to keep doing a work in me.

In 1 Corinthians 10:13 Paul says that God will never allow more to come upon us than we can bear, but with every temptation He will also provide a way out. We can trust God not to expect us to endure beyond our ability.

Believe me, God knows what you are capable of bearing even more than you do. Trust Him and He will bring you through the refining process so that you emerge as pure gold.

Press On Toward the Goal

Not that I have now attained [this ideal], or have already been made perfect, but I press on to lay hold of (grasp) and make my own, that for which Christ Jesus . . . has laid hold of me . . . .

Philippians 3:12

In his writings, Paul often likens the Christian life to a race. (1 Cor. 9:24-27.) Trust the Lord and He will bring you across the finish line. Be determined to press on and to take hold of that for which Christ has taken hold of you. He took hold of you to save you.

Your salvation included many things — not just a home in heaven when you die. Your eternal salvation began the day you were born again, and it will never end. God took hold of you to restore to you what the enemy had stolen from you, but you will need to be determined to have it back.

Don't be passive and expect victory to just fall on you. It does come by the grace of God, and not by our works, but we must actively cooperate with the Holy Spirit each step of the way.

In his book, *The Great Lover's Manifesto*, Dave Grant points out that we never grow when things are easy. We waste away without effort. We human beings are essentially lazy and always searching for the easy way, but in reality, we need some tension in order to stretch and grow. We won't grow until we agree that struggle benefits us and that struggle is good, because it keeps us moving and alive. Paul said that he "pressed on." His phrase indicated tension and struggle; it indicated that the Christian walk is not easy.

In Grant's book, he relates the following story: "A number of bees were taken along on a flight into space in order to see how they would handle the experience of weightlessness. In the weightless atmosphere they were able to float in space without any effort. The report on the experiment was summed up in these words: '*They enjoyed the ride, but they died*'" (emphasis mine).[1] I agree 100 percent with Mr. Grant, who goes on to say that we seldom *drift* into anything worthwhile.

---

[1]*The Great Lover's Manifesto*, copyright © 1986 by Harvest House Publishers, Eugene, Oregon 97402 ISBN 0-89081-481-3, p. 13.

Hang Tough in Hard Times!

Though the fig tree does not blossom and there is
no fruit on the vines, [though] the product of the olive
fails and the fields yield no food, though the flock is
cut off from the fold and there are no cattle in the stalls,

Yet I will rejoice in the Lord; I will exult in the
[victorious] God of my salvation!

The Lord God is my Strength, my personal bravery,
and my invincible army; He makes my feet like hinds'
feet and will make me to walk [not to stand still in
terror, but to walk] and make [spiritual] progress upon
my high places [of trouble, suffering, or responsibility]!

Habakkuk 3:17-19

The Old Testament prophet Habakkuk spoke of hard
times, calling them "high places" and stating that God had
given him hinds' feet to scale those high places.

In case you are not familiar with the term "hind," it
refers to a certain kind of deer that is an agile mountain
climber. It can scale up what looks like a sheer cliff with no
difficulty at all, leaping from ledge to ledge with great ease.

This is God's will for us, that when hardship comes our
way we are not intimidated at all, nor frightened.

To be truly victorious, we must grow to the place where
we are not afraid of hard times but are actually challenged
by them. In these verses *The Amplified Bible* refers to these
"high places" as "trouble, suffering or responsibility." This
is because it is during these times that we grow.

If you look back over your life, you will see that you
never grow during easy times; you grow during hard times.
During the easy times that come, you are able to enjoy what
you have gained during the hard times. This is really a life
principle; it is just the way it works. You work all week,
then you receive your paycheck and enjoy your weekend
off. You exercise, eat right and take good care of yourself,

then you enjoy a healthy body. You clean your house, or basement, or garage, and then you enjoy your neat, clean surroundings each time you walk through them.

I am reminded of Hebrews 12:11: **For the time being no discipline brings joy, but seems grievous and painful; but afterwards it yields a peaceable fruit of righteousness to those who have been trained by it . . . .**

The person who serves God from love does what is right because it is right. He does not do it to inherit any good, though in the end the blessing will not fail him. Seek to be whole in order to give the Lord glory, and in the end, you will enjoy being glorious.

20
Walls or Bridges?

Walls represent protection. We all have a tendency to build our own walls in an attempt to protect ourselves against being hurt. As I have mentioned several times, although I have a very kind and wonderful husband, there are times when he hurts me. I have come to realize that whenever that occurs, every time my husband causes me emotional pain, I erect a wall — I am speaking spiritually — which I hide behind and keep him out.

One of the things the Holy Spirit has taught me is that when we wall others out, we also wall ourselves in. Many people live lonely, isolated lives because they have erected self-made walls to protect themselves. However, the walls become prisons, and they are trapped in bitterness and isolating loneliness.

The walls we erect are there to prevent us from experiencing emotional pain, but we are unable to love unless we are willing to be hurt.

Spending your lifetime trying to avoid pain is more painful than living normally and dealing with each issue as it arises. Jesus is the Healer and will always be available to minister comfort to you in hurtful situations.

I believe the Lord wants me to encourage you right now to take a step of faith and tear down your self-made walls. The thought will probably be frightening, especially if you have been living behind them for a long time. I always like to remember the walls of Jericho. The *King James Version* of Hebrews 11:30 states that "*by faith*" the walls came down. I have to take a step of faith each time Jesus shows me that I have erected walls. I must choose to put my faith in Him as my Protector, rather than attempting to protect myself.

There are several Scriptures in the Bible that promise God's protection. Isaiah 60:18 is one that ministers to me: **Violence shall no more be heard in your land, nor devastation or destruction within your borders, but you shall call your walls Salvation and your gates Praise.**

What this says to me is that salvation through Jesus Christ becomes a wall of protection about me. From the moment I become His, He takes upon Himself the job of protecting me. However, in order to activate the blessings in my life, I must believe that He is watching over me. As long as I continue to reject the Lord's protection, trying to take care of myself, I will continue to live in bondage and misery.

Another wonderful Scripture on the subject of God's protection is Isaiah 30:18: **And therefore the Lord [earnestly] waits [expecting, looking, and longing] to be gracious to you; and therefore He lifts Himself up, that He may have mercy on you and show loving-kindness to you. For the Lord is a God of justice. Blessed (happy, fortunate, to be envied) are all those who [earnestly] wait for Him, who expect and look and long for Him [for His victory, His favor, His love, His peace, His joy, and His matchless, unbroken companionship]!**

Careful study of this verse reveals God as One Who is literally waiting for an opportunity to be good to us, to bring justice into our situations. However, He can do that only for those who are expecting and waiting for Him to do so. Give up the labor of "self-protection" and start allowing and expecting God to protect you.

Let God be God.

As you enter this new realm, by faith, I cannot promise that you will never be hurt, but I can promise that God is "a

God of justice," which means that He will eventually bring balance and will reward you for choosing His way.

Any person who chooses God's way to handle his problems and hurtful situations is destined for great things.

Even as it is written, . . . we are regarded and counted as sheep for the slaughter.

Yet amid all these things *we are more than conquerors* and gain a surpassing victory through Him Who loved us.

Romans 8:36,37

How can we be more than conquerors, and at the same time look like sheep being led to the slaughter? The answer is simple: While it may appear that we are being taken advantage of, that the Lord is not going to rescue us, we are more than conquerors because in "the midst of the mess" we have a *knowing* inside that our God will never leave us nor forsake us and that at exactly the right moment, our deliverance and reward will come.

Bridges Instead of Walls

I have learned to build bridges instead of walls.

One day while I was praying, the Holy Spirit showed me that my life had become a bridge for others to pass over and find their place in God. For many years, I erected only walls in my life, but now where there were walls there are bridges instead. All the difficult and unfair things that have happened to me have been turned into highways over which others can pass to find the same liberty that I found.

As I stated in the first chapter of this book, God is no respecter of persons. (Acts 10:34.) What He does for one, He will do for another, as long as His precepts are followed. If you will follow the precepts that have been outlined in these pages, you will discover the same freedom that I have found. Then you can become a bridge for others to pass over, instead of a wall that shuts them out.

In Hebrews 5:9 Jesus is referred to as "the Author and Source of eternal salvation." He pioneered a pathway to God for us. He became a highway for us to pass over. It is as though He faced a giant forest and went in ahead of us so that when we came along we could drive right through it without having to fight all the elements and the density of the forest. He sacrificed Himself for us, and now that we are benefitting from His sacrifice, He is giving us a chance to sacrifice for others so they can reap the same benefits we enjoy.

Hebrews 12:2 says that Jesus endured the cross for the joy of obtaining the prize that was set before Him. I like to remind myself of that fact when the way seems hard. I tell myself, "Keep pressing on, Joyce, there is joy ahead."

Make a decision to tear down your walls and build bridges. There are many, many people who are lost in their messes and need someone to go before them and show them the way. Why not be that person for them?

Walls or bridges?

The choice is yours.

Beauty for Ashes

The Spirit of the Lord God is upon me, because the Lord has anointed and qualified me to preach the Gospel of good tidings to the meek, the poor, and afflicted; He has sent me to bind up and heal the brokenhearted, to proclaim liberty to the [physical and spiritual] captives and the opening of the prison and of the eyes to those who are bound,

To proclaim the acceptable year of the Lord [the year for His favor] . . . .

To grant [consolation and joy] to those who mourn . . ., to give them an ornament (a garland or diadem) of beauty instead of ashes, the oil of joy instead of mourning, the garment [expressive] of praise instead of a heavy, burdened, and failing spirit. . . .

Isaiah 61:1-3

Not only does the Lord want to turn your walls into bridges, but, as He promises in Isaiah 61:3, he wants to give you "beauty for ashes."

The promises of Isaiah 61 are rich and plentiful. Read them and make a decision not to miss out on a single one. I will be in agreement with you as I pray that every person who reads this book will inherit the promises.

God has done His part by giving us Jesus. I have done my part by acting on the Word of God and obtaining freedom, then writing this book to help you do the same. Now, you do your part by making a quality decision that you will never give up until you have allowed Him to:

Bind up your wounds;

Heal your broken heart;

Liberate you in every area of your life;

Open your prison door;

Give you joy instead of mourning,

a garment of praise instead of a heavy,

burdened and failing spirit;

and

beauty instead of ashes.

Miraculous Conclusion

As I was proofreading the manuscript for this book, God moved in a mighty way and brought deliverance and healing to the relationship between my father and me. I don't believe it is accidental that the conclusion of the story came in time for me to incorporate it into this book.

Although I had forgiven my father, our relationship was still strained and uncomfortable. He had never been able to fully accept responsibility for his acts and face how devastating his behavior was to my life. Through the years, I tried the best I knew how to have some kind of relationship with my parents, but it was a continual challenge.

I tried on two occasions to confront the issue with my father and mother, but neither of these efforts was successful. Each confrontation brought a lot of anger, upset and blame, without any real conclusion. At least the door had been opened and God was working in secret, behind the scenes, even when it seemed that nothing would ever change.

During the past year, God had regularly been dealing with me about the biblical command to "honor your father and mother." (Ex. 20:12.) I must be truthful and say that although I was willing and desired to do so, I was baffled as to how to go about it. I visited them, called them, prayed for them and took them presents, but still the Lord would say to me, "Honor your father and mother." I knew He was trying to show me something, but I could not grasp what it was.

Finally, one evening as I heard again, "Honor your father and mother," I told the Lord I had done everything for them that I knew to do, and did not know what else it was He wanted. Then I heard Him say, "Honor them in your heart," to which I replied, "What can I honor them for?" He showed me that I could honor them and appreciate them, in my heart, for giving me my life, for feeding and clothing me and for sending me to school.

I had been "doing" things for them outwardly, but God looks on the heart. I found it difficult to have fond feelings of appreciation when all I remembered was pain, but after hearing the same thing for a year from the Lord, I knew that it was important, so I did what He said.

I prayed, "Thank You, God, for my parents and the fact that they gave me my physical life. They brought me into the world; they fed me, clothed me and sent me to school, and I honor them for doing so."

I really saw what God was saying, and that moment I truly did appreciate the part my parents had played in my life.

About a week later, an issue arose concerning our newly released national television program, "Life In The Word." I received news that my family members had seen the program, and were urging my parents to watch it. My father and mother asked me what channel they could see the program on, and I realized that I needed to tell them I would be making reference to the abuse in my childhood because God had called me to help people who have been abused and mistreated.

I could not imagine what it would do to them if they tuned in their television and heard me saying, "I come from a background of child abuse." I did not want to hurt them. I felt awful, but what could I do? Knowing that people find it easy to relate to me because I share my background so openly, I went into much prayer, and then called for a family conference with my husband Dave and our children.

We decided that even though letting my parents know that what I was doing could finish what little relationship we had left, I had to follow God's will for my life.

We went to visit them and I shared the truth, telling them that I was not doing it to hurt them, but had no choice if I was to help the people God had called me to help.

I saw the miracle-working power of God!

My father and mother sat there and listened calmly. No anger was displayed; there were no accusations, no running from the truth.

My father then shared with Dave and me how sorry he was for what he had done to me. He said that God knew he was sorry and if there was any way he could take it back, he would. He told me how he was controlled and could not have prevented himself from what he was doing. He said that he had encountered abuse as a child himself, and was acting out of what he had learned and had become accustomed to.

He further shared that he had watched several television programs on abuse and had begun to realize from them how devastating sexual abuse really is.

He released me to share whatever I needed to and told me not to worry about anything. He said he wanted to build a relationship with me and try to be my father and my friend.

My mother, of course, was ecstatic with joy at the thought of being able to have real relationships with her daughter, grandchildren and great-grandchildren.

My husband, Dave, told my dad that it was one of the greatest days in his life. As for me, I'm still pinching myself to see if I'm dreaming or awake.

God is faithful! Dream big dreams, and never stop hoping!

Bibliography

Backus, William, Ph.D. *Telling Each Other the Truth — The Art of True Communication*. Bethany House Publishers, Minneapolis, Minnesota, 1985.

Backus, William and Chapian, Marie. *Telling Yourself the Truth*. Bethany House Publishers, Minneapolis, Minnesota, 1980.

Beattie, Melody. *Co-dependent No More — How To Stop Controlling Others and Start Caring for Yourself*. Harper & Row, Publishers, Inc., New York, New York, by arrangement with the Hazelden Foundation, 1987.

Carlson, David E. *Counseling and Self-Esteem*. Word, Inc., Waco, Texas, 1988.

Carter, Les. *Putting the Past Behind — Biblical Solutions to Your Unmet Needs*. Moody Press, Chicago, Illinois, 1989.

Galloway, Dale E. *Confidence Without Conceit*. Fleming H. Revell Company, Old Tappan, New Jersey, 1989.

Grant, Dave E. *The Great Lover's Manifesto*. Harvest House Publishers, Eugene, Oregon, 1986.

Hart. Dr. Archibald D. *Healing Life's Hidden Addictions — Overcoming the Closet Compulsions That Waste Your Time and Control Your Life*. Vine books, a division of Servant Publications, Ann Arbor, Michigan, 1990.

Holley, Debbie. "The Trickle-Down Theory of Conditional Love," "The Trickle-Down Theory of Unconditional Love." St. Louis, Missouri.

LaHaye, Tim. *Spirit-Controlled Temperament*. Post Inc., © LaMesa, California, for Tyndale House Publishers, Inc., Wheaton, Illinois, 1966.

Littauer, Florence. *Discovering the Real You by Uncovering the Roots of Your Personality Tree*. Word Books, Waco, Texas, 1986.

McGinnis, Alan Loy. *Confidence — How To Succeed at Being Yourself*. Augsburg Publishing House, Minneapolis, Minnesota, 1987.

Saunders, Molly. *Bulimia! Help Me, Lord!* Destiny Image Publishers, Shippensburg, Pennsylvania, 1988.

Solomon, Charles R., Ed.D. *The Ins and Outs of Rejection*. Heritage House Publications, Littleton, Colorado, 1976.

Sumrall, Lester. *Overcoming Compulsive Desires — How To Find Lasting Freedom*. Creation House, Lake Mary, Florida, 1990.

Walters, Richard P., Ph.D. *Counseling for Problems of Self-Control*. Word, Inc., Waco, Texas, 1987.

Webster's II New Riverside University Dictionary. Houghton Mifflin Company, Boston, Massachusetts, 1984.

About the Author

Joyce Meyer has been teaching the Word of God since 1976 and in full-time ministry since 1980. As an associate pastor at Life Christian Center in St. Louis, Missouri, she developed, coordinated and taught a weekly meeting known as "Life In The Word." After more than five years, the Lord brought it to a conclusion, directing her to establish her own ministry and call it "Life In The Word, Inc."

Joyce's "Life In The Word" radio broadcast is heard on over 250 stations nationwide. Joyce's 30-minute "Life In The Word With Joyce Meyer" television program was released in 1993 and is broadcast throughout the United States and several foreign countries. Her teaching tapes are enjoyed internationally. She travels extensively conducting Life In The Word conferences, as well as speaking in local churches.

Joyce and her husband, Dave, business administrator at Life In The Word, have been married for 31 years and are the parents of four children. Three are married, and their youngest son resides with them in Fenton, Missouri, a St. Louis suburb.

Joyce believes the call on her life is to establish believers in God's Word. She says, "Jesus died to set the captives free, and far too many Christians have little or no victory in their daily lives." Finding herself in the same situation many years ago, and having found freedom to live in victory through applying God's Word, Joyce goes equipped to set captives free and to exchange *ashes for beauty.*

Joyce has taught on emotional healing and related subjects in meetings all over the country, helping multiplied thousands. She has recorded over 165 different audio cassette albums and is the author of 20 books to help the Body of Christ on various topics.

Her "Emotional Healing Package" contains more than 23 hours of teaching on the subject. Albums included in this package are: "Confidence"; "Beauty for Ashes" (including a syllabus); "Managing Your Emotions"; "Bitterness, Resentment, and Unforgiveness"; "Root of Rejection"; and a 90-minute Scripture/ music tape entitled "Healing the Brokenhearted."

Joyce's "Mind Package" features five different audio tape series on the subject of the mind. They include: "Mental Strongholds and Mindsets"; "Wilderness Mentality"; "The Mind of the Flesh"; "The Wandering, Wondering Mind"; and "Mind, Mouth, Moods & Attitudes." The package also contains Joyce's powerful 260-page book "Battlefield of the Mind." On the subject of love, she has two tape series entitled: "Love Is..." and "Love: The Ultimate Power."

Write to Joyce Meyer's office for a resource catalog and further information on how to obtain the tapes you need to bring total healing to your life.

To contact the author, write:

Joyce Meyer
Life In The Word, Inc.
P. O. Box 655
Fenton, Missouri 63026
or call:
(314) 349-0303

*Please include your testimony
or help received from this
book when you write.*

Your prayer requests are welcome.

In Canada, please write:
Joyce Meyer Ministries Canada, Inc.
P. O. Box 2995
London, Ontario N6A 4H9

In Australia, please write:
Joyce Meyer Ministries-Australia
Locked Bag 77
Mansfield Delivery Centre
Queensland 4122

or call:
(07) 3349 1200

Books by Joyce Meyer

Don't Dread

Managing Your Emotions

Life In The Word

Life In The Word Journal

Healing the Brokenhearted

Me and My Big Mouth

Prepare to Prosper

Do It Afraid!

*Expect a Move of God in Your Life... **Suddenly!***

Enjoying Where You Are On the Way to Where You Are Going

The Most Important Decision You'll Ever Make

When, God, When?

Why, God, Why?

The Word, the Name, the Blood

Battlefield of the Mind

Tell Them I Love Them

Peace

The Root of Rejection

Beauty for Ashes

If Not for the Grace of God

By Dave Meyer
Nuggets of Life

Available from your local bookstore.

Harrison House
Tulsa, Oklahoma 74153
For additional copies of this book
in Canada contact:
Word Alive • P. O. Box 670 • Niverville, Manitoba
CANADA R0A 1E0

The Harrison House Vision

Proclaiming the truth and the power
Of the Gospel of Jesus Christ
With excellence;

Challenging Christians to
Live victoriously,
Grow spiritually,
Know God intimately.